*The Magic Presence*

# ASCENDED MASTER INSTRUCTION

## "I AM" RELIGIOUS ACTIVITY
### OF THE
## SAINT GERMAIN FOUNDATION

The "I AM" Religious Activity represents the Original, Permanent, and Highest Source of the Ascended Masters' Instruction on the Great Laws of Life, as first offered to the Western World by the Ascended Master Saint Germain through His Accredited Messengers, Mr. and Mrs. Guy W. Ballard.

In the early 1930's, the Ballards established the Saint Germain Foundation and Saint Germain Press, which under Saint Germain's Guidance have expanded into worldwide organizations that offer to mankind the True Ascended Master Teachings on the Great Cosmic Words, "I AM"! The Saint Germain Foundation strives to keep this "I AM" Ascended Master Instruction in Its pure, unadulterated form, free from any human interpretation, personal monetary gain, or any proselytizing, as It is a Gift from the Great Ascended Masters and Cosmic Beings to bring Illumination and Perfection to mankind.

Hundreds of "I AM" Sanctuaries and "I AM" Temples exist throughout the world, where the Teachings are applied in "I AM" Decree Groups. The Books of the Saint Germain Series are available through the Saint Germain Press and in many libraries and bookstores. For further information, please contact:

SAINT GERMAIN FOUNDATION
SAINT GERMAIN PRESS, INC.
1120 Stonehedge Drive
Schaumburg, Illinois 60194

(708) 882-7400          (800) 662-2800

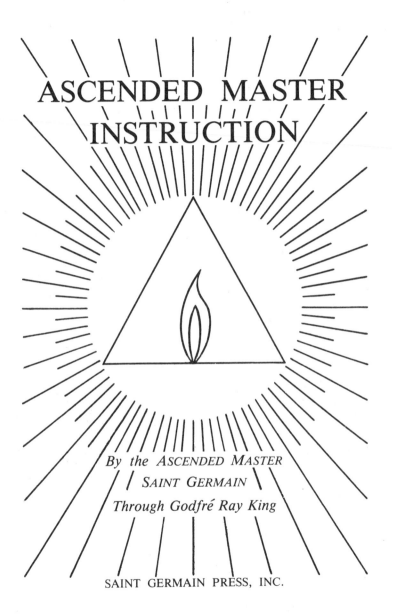

# ASCENDED MASTER INSTRUCTION

*By the ASCENDED MASTER*
*SAINT GERMAIN*
*Through Godfré Ray King*

SAINT GERMAIN PRESS, INC.

TRADEMARKS AND SERVICE MARKS OF THE SAINT GERMAIN FOUNDATION INCLUDE THE FOLLOWING:

Ascended Masters' Instruction of the "Mighty I AM Presence," SM The Ascended Masters' Instruction, SM "Beloved Mighty I AM Presence,"® Daughters of Light,® Honor Cross, TM Honor Cross Design, SM "I AM" SM "I AM" Activity,® "I AM" Angels of Light,® "I AM" Ascended Master Youth, SM "I AM" COME!® "I AM" Emblem,® "I AM" Music of the Spheres,® "I AM" Reading Room, SM "I AM" Religious Activity,® "I AM" Religious Broadcast, SM "I AM" Sanctuary, SM "I AM" School® "I AM" Student Body,® "I AM" Study Groups, SM "I AM" Temple, SM "I AM" Violet Flame, SM The Magic Presence,® "Mighty I AM Presence," ® Minute Men of Saint Germain,® Music of the Spheres,® Saint Germain Foundation,® Saint Germain Press, Inc.® Shasta Springs,® Unfed Flame Design,® Violet Consuming Flame,® Violet Flame,® "Voice of the I AM" ®

Library of Congress Cataloging-in-Publication Data

Germain, Saint (Spirit)
    Ascended master instruction.

    (The Saint Germain series ; v. 4)
    1. I AM Religious Activity.   I. King, Godfré Ray,
1878-1939.   II. Series: Saint Germain series ; v. 4.
BP605.I18G46   1985                    299'.93                    85-19597

ISBN: 1-878891-18-9

# DEDICATION

 T is with the deepest gratitude of our Hearts that we dedicate this Book, *Ascended Master Instruction,* Volume IV, to our own Beloved Mr. and Mrs. G. W. Ballard, whose tremendous obedience, love of the Light, untiring service, and complete devotion to Beloved Saint Germain made these Discourses possible.

These two individuals were the only human beings on the Earth through whom this Mighty "I AM" Ascended Master Instruction could be given; and it is to these Ascended Masters—the Beloved Cosmic Beings Godfre and Lotus—that we dedicate this series of Discourses.

May every human being on Earth who reads this Mighty Ascended Master Instruction also attain the Victory of the Ascension at the close of this embodiment, according to God's Divine Plan for each Life Stream.

## GOD BLESS YOU

# TRIBUTE

E OFFER our Hearts' love and gratitude to Mr. and Mrs. G. W. Ballard, the Accredited Messengers of the Ascended Masters, for their great strength, obedience, and tireless efforts that opened the way to bring this *Ascended Master Instruction* to the world.

When Mr. Ballard had received the experiences as recorded in *Unveiled Mysteries* and *The Magic Presence,* Volumes I and II of the Saint Germain Series, he returned to their home in Chicago where he and Mrs. Ballard began to instruct a small group of Students in the Laws of Life which they had received.

One morning, Mr. and Mrs. Ballard and their son, Donald, were standing near the door to their dining room when they felt a tremendous Vibratory Action charged into the room. Looking up, they saw a Ray of Light descend onto the dining room table. From within this Ray they heard the Voice of the Beloved Ascended Master Saint Germain saying: *"We would like to dictate a series of Discourses, should you care to cooperate. Take time to think it over and let Me know."* Mrs. Ballard answered immediately, *"We are ready to begin now!"* *"Very well,"* Saint Germain replied, *"We will begin next week!"*

Twice a week for over seven months these Mighty Discourses came forth, followed by *The "I AM" Discourses* as published in Volume III of the Saint Germain Series. Mr. Ballard has said concerning this Great Instruction, *"It is the most wonderful thing that ever came into a human being's Life!"*

We wish to explain to the reader that we have included the closing Discourse of Volume III, given by Beloved Mighty Arcturus on July 4, 1932, as the opening Discourse in this Volume. By printing these Discourses in Volume IV in chronological order, we feel that our Beloved Mighty Arcturus and Beloved Mighty Saint Germain can enfold the world in *Their Mighty Violet Flame of Elohim Power and Protection*—forever manifest!

THE EDITORS

# FOREWORD

UR Beloved Ascended Master Saint Germain dictated this series of twenty-eight Discourses over a visible Light and Sound Ray in the home of our Beloved Mr. and Mrs. Guy W. Ballard in Chicago.

This *Ascended Master Instruction* is published from the original manuscripts left by Mr. and Mrs. Ballard. Only fragments of the real Understanding of the "I AM Presence" had been given to the world until this Ascended Master Consciousness came forth. The Beloved Ascended Master Saint Germain says: *"It is the most important Understanding mankind can ever have, and there is no Freedom nor Perfection for the individual except through this conscious Application."*

When the phrase, " 'Mighty I AM Presence,' come forth!" is used throughout this series of Books, it is always a Call to the "God Presence" to pour forth or release the Outpouring of Perfection that the one making the Call desires.

This Book not only carries the Ascended Masters' Understanding of the "Beloved Mighty I AM Presence," but it is charged with Beloved Saint Germain's Ascended Master Consciousness and the

Ray of Light and Love from His Heart, which are His Ascended Master Feeling and Comprehension of its Full Power, forever self-sustained.

May this Book of *Ascended Master Instruction* anchor the attention of all who read or contact it so powerfully upon each individual's own Divinity that the Full Ascended Master Consciousness of the "Mighty I AM Presence" shall fill the Earth—and release with the Power of a Thousand Suns the Eternal Dominion of *"The Light of God that never fails"!*

THE EDITORS

# CONTENTS

# ASCENDED MASTER INSTRUCTION

*By the* ASCENDED MASTER SAINT GERMAIN

## DISCOURSE I

ARCTURUS' INDEPENDENCE DAY DISCOURSE

*July 4, 1932*

SAINT GERMAIN

*INVOCATION:* Mighty Sustaining, Enfolding "Presence"! We give praise and thanks for Thy Life Everlasting, Thy Youth Eternal, Thy Light Illumining.

## *THE DISCOURSE*

ARCTURUS

O America! *We love you!* Mighty Seed of God's Eternal Manifestation, We give praise and thanks that Thou art sustained and governed by God alone. The day on which Independence within Thy Heart was established, Thou didst become a Radiating Center of Light to all humanity. We give praise and thanks that out of all will come peace and prosperity to mankind in Thy Embrace. *Back of Thee is the*

*1*

*Power that will sustain and maintain the Reign of God on Earth.* His Light shall illumine and strengthen the Hearts of Thy Children in all ruling places; and out of all shall come Love, Justice, and Wisdom.

America, We love you! America, We love you! America, We love you! Today, O America, those Mighty Messengers of God who have passed before, look upon Thee with their Hearts filled with Love and Strength, the Love of the "Mighty I AM Presence" flowing forth to heal, to bless, and to prosper Thy inhabitants. The very substance of Earth is being quickened into greater activity; and as the Children of God walk the Earth, so shall they feel the *Current of God* flowing in—quickening them into greater Love, Loyalty, and desire for Thy Freedom. O America! Thou dost seem to have become bound, but Thou art not. Thou art entering into Thy Great Freedom. Thou dost seem in the throes of pain; but Thou wilt be born into that great Peace, Health, Happiness, and Prosperity. We give praise and thanks that this is God's Wisdom—the "Mighty I AM Presence"—speaking.

*The Christ Child enfolding Thee, America, has grown into Majesty and Power. It no longer pleads but commands obedience of all that is of the outer to the service of the Inner "Presence." The Power of*

*Divine Love governs Thee and consumes all unlike Itself.* America! We give praise and thanks that Thou art a Great Jewel within the Heart of God, the Lamp of Illumination lighted by the "Mighty I AM Presence," the Chalice, the Crystal Cup holding within Its pure Radiance the Freedom, Peace, Health, Prosperity, and Illumination of those who dwell within Thy Embrace. May all the World feel Thy Radiance and be blest by It. Peace! Peace! Peace! And on Earth goodwill to man.

ARCTURUS

*Notes:* I would suggest that some time each day you think of yourself as a radio station sending forth peace and goodwill to all mankind. Know that in this Mighty Consciousness, the Limitless Power of the "Mighty I AM Presence" flows forth to each individual and gives that which he or she is ready to receive, bringing enlightenment and decision to everyone. Be conscious that your own minds are such powerful Divine Centers that at any time you can make quick, unerring decisions through the Power of Divine Love. Recognize that your mind is but a vehicle of the Great Master Presence of the "Mighty I AM Presence" within, and that it is to obey that Inner "Presence" at all times. Command it to always act with decision, alertness, and quickness, and that all human sense of wavering be forever consumed.

*The New Cycle:* Today is a focal point of ten thousand years, the beginning of another cycle of ten thousand years in which the Great Ones from Venus, who have always been instrumental in the upliftment of humanity and our Earth, this day come forth and pour out to humanity throughout the Earth a Mighty Radiance. This will bring about more quickly a greater stabilization and confidence in the Hearts of many public officials. It will cause them to have a strong, unwavering desire to reestablish America in confidence and prosperity, and make them feel a deeper love and loyalty for Her progress than ever before.

Many will have learned that they cannot rule humanity with a ruthless hand; for they are seeing that the inroad of control which they had desired to gain over others, is returning to themselves for redemption. If this lesson can be impressed upon them sufficiently, a great calamity will have been averted. In this quickening period, things can be done in the short period of twenty years that would ordinarily require a hundred years.

SAINT GERMAIN'S DESCRIPTION OF THE
NEW YEAR'S EVE CONCLAVE AT THE ROYAL TETON

*January 1, 1935*

It is with Great Joy that I relate to you briefly some
of the Activity that took place at the Royal Teton
last night. Two hundred and fourteen of the Ascended Masters were present and the twelve from
Venus. The All-Seeing Eye was in the most powerful
Action known thus far. Great Rays of Light were
made permanent to our national Capitol and the
capital of each state, so that a constant Radiation
might pour forth to these focal points; and also to
the principal cities of Europe, India, China, Japan,
Australia, New Zealand, South America, Africa,
and Mexico. A similar Activity or Radiation from
the Golden City and Shamballa was also poured
forth, making a Triple Activity for the Blessing of
mankind.

*Every effort is being made to avoid as much de-
structive activity as possible throughout the World.*
The activity of the past three months has been tremendously encouraging, and We do have high expec-
tations for this year. Being so well aware of the Free
Will of humanity, We can but trust in their harmonious cooperation with the Conscious Radiation

pouring forth from the above-mentioned Triple Activity.

*There were Outpourings of Light from the Tall Master from Venus, Jesus, and the Great Divine Director, such as I have not known before in My Experience.* The many who have been fully aware of My sincere Efforts for the Blessing of America have now joined Me in Full Power to achieve all possible that the Cosmic Law and the law of the individual will permit. The Cosmic Laws are daily giving greater freedom in this activity, which is the thing that gives Us such great encouragement.

There were many Students present last night, for which I am very grateful. There is much detail of the Activity which took place that I may not reveal at this time, but I assure all the Students that It was marvelous beyond description.

The Great Host of Ascended Masters join Me in Their Love, Light, Blessing, and Opulence to the Students, to America, and to the World, that this year may be unparalleled in its happiness to mankind.

In the Fullness of My Love,

SAINT GERMAIN

(Reprinted from Volume III)

# DISCOURSE II

*July 7, 1932*

SAINT GERMAIN

*INVOCATION:* Thou "Mighty I AM Presence" from the Heart of the Great Central Sun! We face Thy Sunrise!

## THE DISCOURSE

*Daily exercise:* You may do this at any time during the twenty-four hours. Stand erect, face the east, and say mentally or aloud (be guided by your own feelings as to whether you should say it aloud or not), but let it be firm: *"Mighty God in me! I face Thy Eternal Sunrise and receive Thy Mighty Radiance and Activity visibly manifest in my experience now."* The use of this sets into motion certain powerful principles.

*Warning:* If Students use this, they should analyze themselves first and see if they are really sincere in their determination to have and serve the Light unconditionally. If they be sincere, let them stand to the Light and then go forth. Awake! Stand to the Light and serve only the One Presence of Right and Justice.

Know that God, the "Mighty I AM Presence" in you, governs and controls all unfoldment in Perfect Divine Order. As the sea holds all created Life in its embrace which is designed for its sphere, so the air holds within its embrace those created forms of Life belonging to it. These are two links ever active between the human and the Divine, or the physical and the White Fire Body. We may call upon these forms of Life to give us the best of their element.

Man is the only creator of inharmony. The elements and their inhabitants are always harmonious in themselves, and it is only when one gets out of one's element that inharmony is created; but the inharmony is not of the element itself.

The human element, or outer sphere of mankind, is the only element in Creation that deliberately creates inharmony and consciously misuses the energy of the God sustaining it. This is the only sphere in the Universe where those who function within it have taken command and declared themselves independent of God. I mean by this, those who are refusing to acknowledge the active Presence of God in their lives.

No principle or activity can be blamed for the misuse mankind makes of it. All through the ages, humanity has tried to place upon God the responsibility for its destructive activities. Hence the ruse of manufacturing gods who could be either angry or joyous according to mankind's whim.

I assure you from My own observation, that those Great Ones—far greater than I—through aeons of investigation, have indisputable proof that there is but One God—the Life, Wisdom, and Energy of all Creation. Therefore, the Energy of God cannot be blamed for the inharmony created when someone misuses It. Neither can the principle of banking be blamed because of dishonest bankers. Neither can the activity or principle of giving out information by the press be blamed because of malicious reporters or dishonest editors.

I assure you that the day is not far distant when these principles of activity will be used in their highest constructive power. The constructive, educational moving picture will also be used as the quickest, easiest, and most certain way of educating the outer perception.

Too long has mankind usurped and misused the Energy of good, which is God. The Inner Quickening, by the Cosmic Radiation through the Mighty Arisen Messengers of God into the Heart of each individual, is rapidly drawing the human desire into the Divine. As is the case in all seeming struggles between two forces, so in the conditions of today, they are but the old conditions being repeated. And out of it all will come, for the first time on Earth, a permanently established condition and right attitude of mind in the outer activity of humanity.

I want so much to have each one of the Students keep before them the fact that *they alone* are the governor of their Life and its activity, and are commanded to choose what they wish to manifest in their Life—always remembering that they are not to stop and worry about this or that individualization. They are to fix their vision, which is God's Inner Activity, on the Goal and hold it there with a firm, joyous determination to reach it.

*No advice to others:* Knowing this, there is no one who should attempt to advise another. The God in each is the *only one* who knows what is best for each individual.

Those who are experiencing discordant activity should go where they can be absolutely quiet and uninterrupted; then to the best of their ability, enter into the Great Silence and, as they become quiet, say: " *'Mighty I AM Presence!' I demand to know the right attitude and activity that I should take in adjusting and solving this problem!"* If the Answer does not come at once, each day enter into the Silence again and continue to demand that the Divine Answer come forth. Also demand to be shown, through the Inner Vision, every detail which should be carried out. Then all of a sudden, possibly when most unexpected, will come forth into the outer consciousness the full unquestionable solution to the problem or situation.

*Running away:* As one may not at any time run away from anything, this will make clear to him the complete situation, and reveal whether he is being held by the hypnotic influence or whether he is fulfilling a just obligation.

If I were to unleash My Love for My Students and attempt to advise them, I might be interfering with opportunity of immense value to them. Because I might know a thing, does not permit Me to take away from the Student valuable opportunity. No one should feel distressed or lose hope because of outer conditions, when a few moments' contemplation can but reveal the fact that there is only One Power, Energy, or Activity to use or that is being used — which is God! When one depends upon and demands of this Supreme "Presence" the right solution of any problem or situation, it will be solved or adjusted with the most wonderful Divine Activity. The Divine Solution will far transcend anything the outer mind could conceive of, even if it had the power of accomplishment within itself.

Knowing that the outer mind or consciousness is a mighty vehicle through which the tremendous

Energy of God can be consciously directed, then we
know that we have every moment, all about us, the
most powerful Presence for Protection and Direction, and the Supreme Solver and Adjuster of every
condition that opportunity brings before us. It
would save so much distress to the individual if on
the first intimation of any intruding discord he or
she would leap, as it were, into the Heart of this
Mighty "Presence" and say: *"Seemingly the outer has
made a mistake. I call on Thy Law of Forgiveness.
See that this is adjusted quickly and completely."*

Take a firm grip on the Inner "Presence" to govern every inharmony and to remove any wrong condition permanently. The highest and quickest action
is always to make the Demand to the Great Inner
"Presence." God's Energy always acts according to
the consciousness we have of It. Opportunity is a very
poor master; it is you who must always govern it. Use
opportunity, but never let it use you.

*The Assistance of the Masters:* The Great Ones
may and do give Assistance at all times, whether the
Students know it or not. One of the Greatest Activities of the Ascended Beings which They perform for
the Students, is to give Courage, Strength, and Assurance, until such a time as they make a strong
enough contact with their own Inner "Presence"
to fully and clearly loose Its Mighty Wisdom and

Activity into the outer self.

The result of this Radiation is that the Students build permanent strength of character, and it saves them endless repetition and re-creation of imperfection. In the past, down through the centuries, the Call to the "Mighty I AM Presence" within the individual has been but intermittent. Now the work before each one is to make the contact with the God within and hold it.

The idea is not to ease up as soon as a problem is solved and think that no further effort is required — but to keep calling to this Mighty Inner "Presence," and recognizing and accepting It going before to see that these foolish human problems are consumed at their first intimation. In this way the Divine Self keeps you free from the outer disturbing or binding conditions.

Experience is but opportunity and is one of the most powerful friends the outer self has; for it gives the outer a chance to bring forth the Divine Character of Life, which knows no imperfection. Allow Me to say again: " *'Mighty I AM Presence!' Reveal to me Your True Solution of this situation in which I seem to be concerned. Come forth in Your Wisdom and Strength and solve this in Divine Order without another moment's delay. I recognize that You do not need time, place, nor space, but that Your All-*

*powerful Activity is now! I accept this fact."*

*Explanation of Cosmic Karma:* I wish to put before the Students another very vital and important thing, which concerns human creation. The individual can call on the Law of Forgiveness and say to the "I AM Presence," *"Dissipate and consume this wrong creation."* This throws it back to the Cosmic Law for adjustment, wherein it is adjusted outside of the individual karmic activity.

There are a great many individuals to whom this idea of Truth would give immense relief and great Freedom in a very short time. I cannot stress too strongly how the individual, being the only creator of inharmony, can, by the conscious Application of the Law of Forgiveness, remove forever from his or her individual activity a great deal that would be very distressing.

The old idea of karma—an eye for an eye and a tooth for a tooth—has not been correctly understood, except by a few. The majority have thought that karma must be balanced individual to individual. In some cases this is imperative; but there is so much that does not have to be balanced in that way, when the correct idea of it is understood.

One of the unfortunate things when the idea of karma was advanced, was the above mistake. It caused individuals to consciously bind themselves to each other for adjustment. Taking into consideration that each individual has Free Will, you can see how this individual-to-individual balancing might become an endless thing. If one individual be not in a mood to cooperate in the adjustment of a condition, how then could the activity ever be ended? There must be and is a wiser means of help to do it. If the above material is carefully contemplated by the Students, they will find greater relief and peace from realizing that they have this Wise "Presence" upon which they may call in all conditions.

*BENEDICTION*: We give praise and thanks that shortly Thy Messengers will fill every office in this Land, and that the Reign of God is now manifest on Earth.

## DISCOURSE III

*July 11, 1932*

SAINT GERMAIN

*INVOCATION:* Thou Mightiest of the Mighty, Thou Mighty God! We face Thy Sunrise! These Thy Children face the Sunrise of the Soul and receive Thy All-sustaining Power, Thy Courage, Thy Wisdom, and Thy Illumining Presence. Thou Mightiest of all Energy! We accept Thy Presence. Thou All-powerful, Active "Presence" animating our minds and forms, Thou Mighty Intelligence! We accept Thy All-powerful Activity directing every movement of the outer form, holding it close in Thy Mighty Embrace.

### THE DISCOURSE

*God's Certain Assurance:* In every activity of Life, there must be something to which the consciousness can be anchored or which can stabilize it. In the outer mind there are principles and formulas that it may use in coming to a definite conclusion. For instance, by following the principles of mathematics, we come to certain results. When a formula is worked out, you produce certain results — no question about it. How much more important it is then to get the attention of the individual fixed upon that Indwelling "Presence" with the same assurance. You must know that the Principle of Life in you and enfolding you, is far greater than the outer things which you have experienced for long centuries and have unknowingly clung to.

May I remind you of what I gave on July 7? Do the following any time during the waking hours: Stand, face the east, and say verbally or mentally — but let it be firm: *"Mighty God in me! I face Thy Eternal Sunrise and receive Its Mighty Radiance and Activity, visibly manifest in my experience."* Follow your feeling as to whether you say it verbally or mentally each time. You will find that this produces certain results, the nature of which I may not speak of, in order that you may receive the full benefit. If Students use this, they should first analyze themselves and see if they are sincere in their stand to the Light. If they are sincere, let them stand to the Light and then go forth! The Principle of God, which is your active consciousness, is always enfolding the outer form. It is the Mightiest of Principles that the outer self may be aware of and cling to.

By doing this you can have the same certain,

definite results, with the same great assurance of success that you receive in the use of other principles or formulas in mathematics or chemistry. The Master "Presence" in you *is* the Mightiest of Chemists and the Greatest of all Principles or Formulas.

All seeming shadows or problems are but a part of God demanding an opportunity for the recognition of that Great and Mighty "Presence," the Invincible Solver of all problems. All problems are but to compel a recognition of God as the Supreme Controller and Activity in all things.

This Mighty "Presence" is the certain assurance, anchored in the Heart of every individual on the Pathway of Light, that he may definitely and absolutely Ascend. Therefore, you will see that the outer experience, which would otherwise seem disconcerting or disturbing, is but the Demand of the Great Self to the outer to turn about and *face the Eternal Sunrise of God's Glorious Radiance* enfolding every one of His Children and all His Creation. As you contemplate this fact, every earnest Soul will feel the Radiance of this Mighty Truth strengthening and sustaining him with a Joyous Presence in every experience through which he may pass.

In presenting this Mighty Sustaining Truth from various angles, it is done with the certain consciousness that one angle or another will meet the requirements of the Students in various grades, enabling each one to grasp his Principle of Life, the "Mighty I AM Presence" — the God within — with certain, definite assurance. Each one will recognize his own God Principle working in him and for him, and he will feel his certain ability to apply It in his own Life and problems.

I wish to make clear that when We say, "the Principle of God within," I do not mean to convey, nor has it ever been intended to convey that the Great Principle of God dwells within the outer form; but Its Wondrous *Radiation* can be and is often felt within the outer form. The Golden Thread of Light, anchoring the Mighty Master Self within the Heart and brain of the outer form, is the Mighty Current or Stream of Life by which the outer is sustained and given its activity. This can be drawn upon and used with positive assurance concerning the desired results, and Its Mighty Energy can be used without any limit.

When Students can feel the assurance of this, their Freedom is at hand; and at this point again let Me state the importance to the Students of the Command, *"To hear, to dare, to do, and to be silent."* This particularly concerns Instruction. If earnest Students allow themselves to discuss Instruction with other Students who may or may not have the same viewpoint, it will many times cause them to waver and be deprived of the great recognition and acceptance that they might otherwise utilize.

Each Student receiving Instruction should contemplate that Instruction and refuse to discuss It with anyone other than his or her Teacher. This will many times help them avoid very grave confusion. Only after Students have become firmly anchored in the Truth, are they able to enter into the discussion of the various angles of Truth without experiencing confusion. This is why Students in the Retreats of the Ascended Masters, as a rule, make such remarkable progress. The Students in the outer world can have the same unvarying results if they will generate strength within themselves and resist the temptation of discussing the Truths that are most Sacred to them and others. As no one individual may grow for another, then it is obvious when the Student is receiving Instruction, that he or she is but wasting energy in the outer discussion.

Contemplation of the Instruction or the Truth given, will enable the individual to receive the proof from within, that the words are intended to convey. The Student, to become safely anchored, must at all times look to the Mighty Master "Presence," God enfolding him, for the right solution of every problem confronting him. Except where worded Instruction is being given him, the Student should at all times look to the Mighty "Presence" within and hold his attention there, firmly fixed, until the Answer to any question he requires appears. When the sincere Student looks with earnest determination to the Master "Presence" enfolding him, he will have at his service the Mightiest Forces of the Universe; and this will cause those Mighty Forces to rush to his assistance whatever is required. Earnest Students who do this will not long be affected by outer conditions.

All the inhabitants of the Elements are subject to the qualities given them because of the racial conception of fairies and Angels. Fairies and sylphs are both inhabitants of the air, but different activities of it. The outer consciousness of human beings constantly jumps to conclusions. If Angels or Arisen Beings were to manifest to perform a visible physical or tangible action, They would necessarily project a form. If it were Protection or Inspiration, They might appear as a Flame, or a Ball of Light. The outer self always wants proof and so causes the "Presence" to project that which is tangible.

Every Student should understand that every condition he meets in the outer returns back to him the qualities he gives it — hence the necessity of seeing, knowing, and feeling only *God in Action* in every situation. The Great Law, when It strikes a certain point of Activity, always finds Its Way to accomplish a thing that is needed for a given purpose. The motive is always the judge back of every outer activity.

Where Students have been taught the gratification of sex as a necessity, on leaving the body they are met by Those who have the correct knowledge and who correct that idea and give the help needed. The human self or outer consciousness is terrifically stubborn.

*Cremation:* Cremation not only disintegrates the physical body, but it also consumes the destructive element of the emotional or astral body and looses the desire in the individual to be taught. The emotional or astral is partly physical because all atomic structure comes within the physical domain. The Electronic Structure is beyond the physical domain. Many times the release from the physical leaves the consciousness clearer to receive the Light. It is true that those who are antagonistic to the Truth here are not necessarily so after passing on.

Students should be absolutely certain within themselves that no amount of hate, gossip, criticism, or condemnation of the outer can harm them. If — on becoming aware of any such thing — they know there is only God acting, they transmute the condition, and that force is used for their own benefit.

So it is with the force released by the hate and

explosions of the First World War — 1914-1918. It is constantly being requalified and redirected to be used for good. When a force is released, it is neither good nor bad; it is simply energy that can be directed. *Force is always qualified by the consciousness or individual using it.*

When the explanation of the Sayings of the Master Jesus is given at the point we are at today, it is curious what Tremendous Strength and Power were in the Statements He made — showing what a Powerful Condensation They were.

The comparison of the outer principles to the Inner will often enable the Students to grasp and apply the Inner with even more definite assurance than they are able to apply the outer.

" *'I AM' the Divine Plan of the Light in physical operation.* "

# DISCOURSE IV

*July 14, 1932*

SAINT GERMAIN

*INVOCATION:* God, Thou Central Source of all Activity, Wisdom, and Power, We demand Judgment now, that those of Thy Children looking to Thee may find Thy Radiance enfolding and governing their minds, bodies, homes, and every activity. We demand Thy Judgment be now, and that every Heart that looks to Thee may find itself enfolded in Thy Unconquerable Radiance. Shed forth such Power that nothing may touch the world of these individuals but Thy Perfect Activity; for We recognize that out of the Fullness of Thy Presence comes the Perfect Manifestation, the visible Presence of all things — and so it is decreed.

## THE DISCOURSE

Today is an opportunity to prove the atmosphere of God [the day was very hot]. Concentrate the attention on the region of the pineal gland, knowing that the attention focused there will cause to take

place the balancing activity of all the centers, drawing and giving all power to the head center. From
this center, the power of speech—which is but
thought representation—will reflect back to the vo-
cal center.

During this time of the contemplation, or conscious direction of the attention to the Highest
Center, be aware of the even, balanced, rhythmic
breath. I do not mean to give it special attention,
but breathe a few times consciously, and then just
be conscious that you are breathing the rhythmic
breath. Breathe in on a count of eight; hold for eight
counts; breathe out on eight, and hold eight. Then
repeat. After doing this a few times you will get the
rhythm near enough. The activity of this consciousness responds to the demand.

The great God Principle is above and enfolding
the form because of the Anchorage of God within
the Heart. The Seven Centers are the Points of Anchorage of the Individualization of God in the physical form. The pineal gland is the Point of Anchorage
and Radiation of the Great Central Sun. When we
realize this, we have come to the point where we do
not consider any of the lower centers.

Keep asking the God within what the correct activity is to use at a specific time. Each must depend
on the direction he receives from the God within

himself. All instruction is but worded attention upon certain things, and the Student should learn from the words instead of the presence of the one giving it. The Radiation will come through the words themselves; the words are but vehicles of conveyance of the "Presence." The feeling and thought will become just as accurate as the spoken word, as you depend more and more on the Presence of God.

It is necessary to use the Consuming Flame at least once a day. It is especially necessary among the Students because some unknowingly open themselves to discordant things due to mass pressure.

In the use of the Rays, try to feel with intensity the Mighty Presence of God there, operating in whatever color you use.

*Very important—Divine Love:* Keep the attention on the fact that Love is the Controlling Power in all conditions, always knowing it is Divine Love. This qualifies whatever human love is there and raises it in harmony with Divine Love. *Know always that in any Demand God is the Sustaining Power.* You must keep aware of this fact in the use of all Law. Remember that in all conscious use of the Law, *you are at all times the determiner of the qualities you wish manifest and maintained!* No two individuals are affected exactly alike; one has an irritation of mind, another of body, another anxiety, another impaired health.

The constant consciousness that *"God is my Perfect Health, Wealth—and is Self-sustained,"* will take one into the full visible manifestation of these conditions. Know: *"God in me is the Keeper of my Treasure House; then I know God produces in my visible use, great abundance, money as fast as I require its use, and that it is never late and that all my seeming obligations are taken care of on time."* The joyous indifference of youth is really a letting go; and with Love prevailing, it is the most potent Power for Manifestation.

*To Mrs. G. W. Ballard: Never let down your bars of protection to anyone.* It is wise for all to use the consciousness that God's Activity is in this home and all about it, and there is only God acting. In thinking of the neighbors, know that God governs their every activity in regard to this home. Take a thing in the beginning, and with intensity reverse the negative action in thought and feeling concerning it. The seemingly deeper acceptance of the negative instead of a positive condition in the human consciousness, is a mental gravity pull and is due to the density of the physical substance of the body.

*A quick forceful statement: "No, you get out of here! God Almighty is in control."* This is true up to a certain point of Illumination: while the Inner "Presence" always stands ready to act, the consciousness of invitation within the Student's outer mind seems to be imperative. The Inner "Presence" does not intrude Itself; It must be invited.

The nature of the outer consciousness is to swing from one extreme to the other. The Eternal Balance is "the Middle Way"; and the desire to move in that activity, draws and holds you there. The desire to walk "the Middle Way" draws you and holds you in it. The deeper the recognition and living in the "God Presence," the quicker will the God Power act.

*Electronic Activity:* Wherever there is force, there is always some point of Electronic Activity, and from the higher standpoint it is very noticeable. The force released by the World War is still standing in the Earth's atmosphere, and is and will be redirected and used constructively.

The Electrons in our atmosphere are the Emanation from the Great Central Sun. The White Fire Body of the "Mighty I AM Presence" and Its natural Element qualify the Electronic Activity, the same as each Element in itself qualifies the Electronic Activity. The Electron is a Universal Element that is the Spirit of God. Therefore, each Element applying or using the Electron qualifies it according to the Element's own sphere or activity.

In the condensation at a former time—one on Atlantis and the other in the buried cities of the

Amazon—one was a Consuming Activity and the other was a Life-giving Activity. All consuming is but a re-ordering of the balancing of the atomic activity. The Electronic Activity is always permanently balanced within Itself. All discord is but a loss of balance of a particular element or atom. It is only when the electron becomes clothed in a quality that discord is possible. The first activity of the atomic structure is the requirement of something to qualify it, or a need for a quality. Otherwise, it too would remain forever perfect, and no other quality could be imposed upon it.

*Question:* "Why does air in motion seem cooler than still air?"

*Saint Germain:* Because the vibratory action is raised.

The Mantle of Invisibility can be thrown around one instantly, but the Students should establish It permanently and consciously by the practice of visualizing the Mantle around them. We are consciously qualifying this Electronic Energy or Activity every moment.

Instinct is a lower form of intuition. There is only One Presence and Power acting everywhere, so really there are only different grades of consciousness and activity. Words are very lame to carry a meaning that is a feeling.

*The Cross-of-Christ Currents:* Recently there have

been placed Divine Currents in North America in
the shape of a cross or, in other words, in the shape
of a sword; for in this case the Cross of Christ is the
Sword of Currents. The crossbar comes just south of
the Canadian border, the hilt going up into Canada;
and the point reaches south, almost to the lower part
of Florida. Chicago comes at the strong part of the
blade, just below the hilt. These are Currents that
have been placed through the Earth by Mighty Messengers of God.

There will come a time when this Sword and
another will cross, and Peace and Prosperity will be
in America. Where the two Swords come together,
the crossing will be almost over Chicago. These Currents are placed above and within the Earth itself.
They penetrate about one hundred feet below the
surface of the Earth and about two hundred feet
above. This is why the surface structure of the Earth
will change; and the very ground human beings walk
on, will be the Sword of Christ.

In Nature's formation of silver some of it is dense,
and some of it is frosted and not dense. So it is with
the Earth: as the Christ Force is liberated, the Earth
itself will become much less dense. The atmosphere
of the Earth will become the balance between cold
and hot — or semi-tropical — and the moisture will be
evenly distributed. In the new Christ Activity that is

taking place, certain Dispensations are given; but to what extent They will be given has not yet been shown. There are times and points of activity where Dispensations have been given that have advanced civilization hundreds of years.

*Miscellaneous Affirmations:* " 'I AM' God's Child *and I can do everything God wants me to do, and I do it now."*

*"I clothe every atom of my world this day with Infinite Love and Wisdom."*

*"This home is the Heart of Divine Love's Operation."*

*"My body is the Heart of Divine Love's Operation."*

*"My mind is the Heart of Divine Love's Operation."*

*"My world is the Heart of Divine Love's Operation."*

*" 'I AM' the Divine Plan of the Light in perfect physical operation now and forever."*

Be as faithful as you can to healing physical distress, but keep your Inner Eye on the healing of the wounds of hate.

God within you is alive. Do not allow Him to be silenced by thought-forms of your sense perceptions or fears. Always remember that God and His Manifestation are One.

Everything grows by use. All things move in cycles. When the Cosmic Hour strikes, the whole combined Force of the Ascended Host can be used to accomplish a definite Purpose. There are a great many things in which They may not interfere between those periods; otherwise humanity would not be where they are today. When individuals look to Us, We may give Assistance without limit according to their readiness to demand; but in the Cosmic Cyclic Action, We may not interfere.

The night before any important action or before Class, always go into the Secret Heart of God's Great Love. Mankind and Students do not prepare the way ahead. When one wakes in the night, one sometimes returns to the body to anchor in the outer consciousness something that is needed there, or that is to be called forth when a future need arises.

When we come to a certain point of achievement in the prevailing activity, we sometimes make contact with Wisdom gained in previous, forgotten experiences; and if there is a necessity, we call that Wisdom forth and use it. In most instances it is done unknown to the outer consciousness. If we require knowledge that we have been conversant with in previous, forgotten experience, it is many times easier to recall that knowledge than to reach into the Central Source and bring it forth from the uncreated. The

Great Law is not stingy, but it is conservative. It does not permit any unnecessary use of Itself.

*The Divine Record:* Within the Divine Record of every individual there is registered all constructive experience. Therefore when a necessity requires it and the Wisdom is there to be used, naturally that is the first place to draw from. For instance, if you had a book giving certain formulas of activity, you would not go to another individual who had the same kind of book, but you would look into your own book and save the time and energy. If mankind had not forgotten the Wisdom and Force stored within their consciousness, they would much more readily call upon that which is already at hand.

In all the Universe there is no wasted energy, except in the outer activity of mankind. It is not that the Universe can be in any way depleted, but in order that the Student may be taught the conservative use of that Mighty Energy. As the Student goes deeper and deeper into this Great Wisdom, this will become more and more apparent.

*The smell of sulphur:* Mrs. Ballard asked why the smell of sulphur was so strong in the night when there seemed to be no physical cause for it.

It is a Cosmic Process now taking place, and We direct certain Force while you are out of the body, in the Assistance of the Cosmic Activity. The force released by Cosmic Activity through volcanic activity is a force that can be consciously directed. Those who are qualified for this particular activity while yet retaining their physical bodies, are many times instructed how to use this force when out of the body during sleep—especially when a focus of it is required. The outer sense of odor is the conscious memory of the Activity which has already taken place at the Inner Levels. One is likely to smell the odor of wood, sulphur, coal, or incense. If the memory is of sulphur or wood, it is proof that the direct activity of the Highest Force within the Earth was specifically required.

*Raising the vibratory action:* Do not let the outer senses form a habit or get the consciousness of anything except that all raising sensation comes in a perfect, harmonious, natural way. Release a person after treatment into the Wisdom and Activity of God, knowing that It is directing the controlling of the outer mind. When individuals are not aware of how to raise the body, it is sometimes much better to let them get out of the ruined temple and be free to go on.

*For the Groups to use for universal service:* "*The Mighty Power of Divine Love and Justice is now Allpowerfully operating in the minds and outer activity of every one of God's Children in Chicago, New York,*

*America, India, and China. America will again at-tain the Mighty Focus, or Spiritual Power that She once had.*" This Instruction comes from the Ascended Light, and They prefer that no individuality be considered.

Let each one meditate within himself, and then decide upon the particular Ascended Master to whom he wishes to direct his attention, and keep this a secret within his own Heart. The Highest of Attainment is always to look to the God within; and if you need help — assistance of any kind — call to One of the Arisen Host.

# DISCOURSE V

*July 18, 1932*

SAINT GERMAIN

*INVOCATION:* Infinite, "Mighty Presence"—
God Individualized on the sphere of Earth, We give
praise and thanks!

## THE DISCOURSE

*The Ascension:* I bring Greetings from the
Ascended Host and that Master of Masters who sends
Love and Riches to you today. Under this Radiating
Presence, let us consider the meaning and activity of
the word "Ascension." Let us try to dispel the many
misinterpretations of orthodox interpretation. When
the individual has become aware of and, with conscious effort, directs the attention to the region of
the head where the Anchor of the Great Central Sun
is located, he has ascended to the Mount of True
Understanding. This is often referred to symbolically
by the phrase, "going up into the Head Mountain"
—which is often physically true, and yet but symbolizes the fixing of the consciousness on the highest

of the Seven Centers that are the vortices of Activity of the Great Central Sun in man and the Universe.

*The meaning of Satan and evil:* The gross misunderstanding of what Satan and evil really mean is appalling. Many names have been given to this so-called majestic presence of evil, but I assure you that that majestic presence is but a myth. The words "devil," or "sheol," both really came from the word "Satan"; and the root of this word, its true underlying meaning, is "to turn away from that which is inharmonious." The human side of mankind, so to speak, which is never ready to face the Truth of its own being, had to produce some concoction on which to lay the blame of its own creation. The word "Satan" came forth as a single explanation, telling humanity that they had better turn away from their own creations of inharmony, and this turning would enable them to find God ever active in their midst.

Then again there came a time when they wanted still something else to blame for their own wrong creations, and they brought the defenseless serpent into the garden. The serpent but represents a wrong use of the Solar Energy from the Great Central Sun within mankind. This Solar Energy is a most dynamic power and is always active.

Again let us repeat that mankind, having Free Will, are commanded to choose how they shall direct this energy. If they do not direct it consciously for some good, constructive purpose, it will act in some manner — often through the suggestion of the environment or individuals, because energy is always subject to suggestion. The great mass of mankind who have joined themselves to the orthodox idea, as we term it, have thought to cast upon God, a Being in the skies, their problems or creations. Yet they are foolish enough to think they can go on creating inharmony and not experience its discordant effects.

Thus we see how mankind has held over its own head this cloud of ignorance through the centuries. Human beings might have recognized their freedom as Children of God and become conscious of the fact that they had Free Will. They would then have realized that they were the only creators of good and evil, so-called. They would have learned that they had the power to dissipate any wrong or inharmonious creation that they had ignorantly or willfully brought forth.

One of the reasons why the idea of a devil was conceived, was that in every period or cycle of human embodiment, there have been those individuals who were very dynamic in the use of this energy; they were misdirecting it and producing this so-called evil. Besides this, they were creating such powerfully charged thought-forms that vicious, ignorant, disembodied intelligences seized upon them or, as it were, entered into these thought-forms. These forms were being energized by their creators who were still embodied, giving these vicious, ignorant entities tremendous power and activity. Before the time of Jesus, these entities were often able to appear visibly, often in very grotesque forms. Thus, this was the idea of a devil, which I assure you never was and never will exist outside of man's own discordant creation.

*Saints:* A Saint may or may not be an Ascended Being. When Sainthood is conferred on someone, thousands and hundreds of thousands of minds are focused upon this idea or form of a Saint, for there is no idea of a Saint without the form in the mind. Thus, a thought-form of tremendous power is created. Sometimes the Soul of this Saint, through the direction of a great Intelligence, takes advantage of this tremendous creation and enters into the form, producing Miracles of great good. Fortunately, the predominating and balancing thought force in such a creation is always for good. Consequently the Saint, being good, prevents the energy in the thought-form from being used for a wrong purpose. In this thought-form, certain attributes and powers are supposed to be within its domain. The individual furnishes the tremendous energy which is generated to do specific things.

However, when we realize that the Energy of God within the individual is omnipresent, waiting to be consciously directed, we know that in this way it can do far more powerful things than any thought-form. Here is a mystery which has not been explained: Often where a great purpose is to be gained, one of the Great Masters will take charge of this thought-form and produce great and lasting good. Thus, you will see that the energy or force which might have been misused, is often used by wise Intelligences for the accomplishment of great good. It is the privilege of every one of God's Children to do exactly this same thing. Every Student who is sincerely looking to the Light—God, if that one be tripped up, as it were, by his outer self having generated great force through anger or passion—he has the power to re-qualify this energy he has released, and make it work for lasting good. Otherwise it whirls on its way creating discord wherever it goes.

Thus, I tell you in all sincerity that every one of God's Children is a God in embryo and may learn to consciously direct this mighty energy to perform far greater wonders than any Saint has been able to do. The idea of a devil has created appalling ignorance and superstition. Superstition has charged the outer self with such fear that it has paralyzed, so to speak, the very avenues that would lead to its freedom. There is no devil in the Universe except mankind's own inharmonious thoughts and feelings, individual and en masse.

*After the Master Jesus' Ascension:* After the time of Beloved Jesus' Appearance and Ascension, there were those diametrically opposed to the Wondrous Light He had taught and radiated. These were known as forces of darkness. They had gone deep enough into the understanding of the Inner Laws of their being to find that they had certain power of thought, and that they possessed tremendous energy which they could direct for right or wrong, as they chose. These became known at that time, and have been down through the centuries, as black magicians. At one time — I shall not say when — there was a school of these black magicians that set upon and snared, as it were, those Students of Light who had failed to go beyond a certain point of enlightenment. Many times they drew the Student into the full activity of their understanding. On the other hand, there were many in whom the Presence of the Light was strong enough to throw off the influence of these black magicians — after a struggle, the Students were left to go their way.

It was the observation of this activity taking place that drew the attention of the Great Ascended

Masters of Light to this school, and it was broken up and scattered. Since that time it has never been allowed to form a focus of more than two or three individuals in one place. Previous to this time these black magicians created powerful thought-forms which they operated at any distance. Thus was created great havoc and distress during the two closing periods of Atlantis and Egypt; and in fact, they were the underlying causes of all periods of great destruction. Why? Because, aside from their own power to generate destructive force, they utilized the destructive force generated by mankind—thus causing the destruction of an entire race or continent.

*Cause for great encouragement:* Since the time of Jesus' Advent or Appearance upon Earth, these black magicians have never been allowed to form such powerful points of focus wherein a great number of them are gathered together. The tables were turned on them, and among their number were found those whom the Ascended Masters saw wanted to turn from the darkness to the Light. One by one, these were freed from the clutches of the forces of darkness. They became great Exponents of the Light because they were conversant with every subtle activity of the wrong direction of this mighty energy of God. Thus is the great transmutation going on. This is why we feel encouraged that some of the destructive force that at times seemed very near succeeding, might be dissipated, and much cataclysmic activity avoided.

The Tremendous Outpouring of the Christ Activity into the Hearts and minds of mankind since 1884, has enabled many great and wonderful things to be done, which previous to that time might not have been possible. So everyone fortunate enough to receive these Ideas should have courage to go on with a brave Heart, knowing that these days every cloud has its Golden Lining, and back of it—*the Crystal Cup, Pure Light of Christ, God in Action!*

*A Marvelous Promise:* No matter how threatening the storm clouds appear to be, those who stand firm and unyielding to the Light, to the Mighty Individualized Christ Presence, will find their brave Hearts rewarded. They will experience the Golden Lining of these clouds; and before them will appear the Crystal Cup, filled to overflowing with the Mighty Love, Peace, Light, Wisdom, and Abundance of God forevermore. Such a promise, I assure you, is not imaginary, and one day will be fulfilled for all those who stand staunch and true to the Mighty Master "Presence," their own Inner God Self.

The True Ascension of the individual starts long before the raising of the body. As was often represented, Initiation—the Seven Steps of the Ascension were the Seven Steps one takes when mounting from one center to another within the human form. When one has become aware of this fact and has reached the point of understanding where his attention is fixed upon the Highest Center within his head, and when he lives to It accordingly, he has passed his greatest struggle in the raising of the outer form into the Divine. From this point on, he is given much more Assistance — most of which he is entirely unaware of in his outer mind. To become conscious of a Goal of Attainment, knowing that it is not only possible but that it is certain of accomplishment, enables one to look upon the trials of the outer self with great fortitude, courage, and strength, knowing that they are but dust particles flitting before the outer vision.

*Fearing problems:* The reason why problems become rampant, as it were, is because the problem or situation becomes charged with fear by the individual. This gives it a certain powerful activity. One should really strive for just the opposite activity by withdrawing all power from it. Fear is feeling, and feeling is always a vitalizing energy. There are two different kinds of feeling that vitalize tremendously, and these are fear and hate. Instead of giving power to a problem and thus vitalizing it, one should withdraw all sustaining energy and leave it helpless.

The fact of the matter is that all of these problems, so-called, are creations of the outer mind or of laws set up by mankind through the outer self. Through these human laws, people harass each other or try to compel one individual to do for another what he or she is apparently not able to do, because it is the outer, man-made laws acting instead of the Divine. If every individual would turn with all sincerity and ask God's Love and Wisdom to direct him or her every moment and live it accordingly, in less than a year — possibly six months — there would not be a problem confronting mankind.

When you want something fulfilled, it is well to affirm it; but it is also good to write it out and say, *"God! the 'Mighty I AM Presence'! see that this is fulfilled!"* If at any time you seem to have made a mistake, always take this stand and say that only good can come out of it. Know always that God directs your every decision with Wisdom and that you do decide quickly and correctly the Perfect Thing to do and then do it.

*The Great Presence, Surya:* Beloved Surya, who is the same as the Lord Maitreya, is a Great Intelligence from the Great Central, Spiritual Sun; and He will soon begin His Activity on Earth again. Surya is an independent Focus like Cyclopea and the Lords of the Flame from Venus. His Activity is independent because the Assistance He offers is of His own volition and entirely independent of the Hierarchy who have charge of this Planet's growth. He watches over and gives Assistance to all who are nearing the point of the Ascension. He is permitted to intensify that at a given point. At your New Year's Meeting, again there will be your point of contact with this Great Being and the commencement of your Activity with Him as once before.

The "Lodge of Sirius" is really a Cosmic Initiation.

It seems apparent now that on July 4, 1933, there will come very marked changes, for it is of special importance to this government. The Balls of Light sent to certain cities on this Earth, July 1, 1932, from the Royal Teton, were sent to special places in the absence of sufficient physical channels to do certain work in the government. These were sent to New York, Chicago, Alexandria, Hong Kong, and Buenos Aires. Small ones were sent to the capital of every state in America.

Try to keep deep peace in the home, and it will make it possible for Higher Instruction to come forth. At a former period in China, there was instilled into the Chinese race a calm, poised, and silent attitude. Many times this attitude comes from great Adoration of the Supreme "Presence." This characteristic has lasted well into the present day in China; but since the race's contact with the English-speaking people, it has lost a great deal of this quality. The wheels of progress never stop for nations, mankind, or conditions, because the very Activity of God is a forward movement under the direction of those *Mighty Messengers of God*, most of whom have not been heard of on Earth.

*Beloved God Tabor:* The God, "Tabor," referred to in the manuscripts is one of these Great Beings who were actively present during the reign of King David; and the "Mount Tabor" referred to during that period was the Abode of this Great Being.

*Pillar of Fire:* The Ray of Force from the Great Central Sun, which you saw and are visualizing, is a *Pillar of Fire* and is hollow. It has formed a permanent anchorage in the Earth, so that through It there is a constant pouring forth of a Mighty Stream of Purifying Energy. From this explanation, you will see and understand how very important your efforts are. Be sure to keep them up. You are the determiner of what you do, so ask your "Mighty I AM Presence" to see that you do have time to do it and keep this up. This Work must be done!

If anything occurs within the consciousness that causes the least fear or disturbance, one should instantly remember one's "Mighty I AM Presence" —

the Master within — and ask It to dissipate all fear, its cause and its effect at once, and see that it never touches one's being or world again. Why should Students of the Light be harassed by disturbing elements or conditions? Students of the Light who serve the Light, should demand from the Light, Freedom from every disturbing condition!

# DISCOURSE VI

*July 21, 1932*

SAINT GERMAIN

*INVOCATION:* Thou Mighty Ascended Jesus Christ, Individualized Presence within each one! We give praise and thanks for Thy Wondrous Activity every moment of the day—that Thou art the Consciousness lifting mankind out of the dross of the human mind. We give praise and thanks that the Mighty Ascended Host manifest, visibly and invisibly.

We bring Greetings of Love, Joy, Health, and Prosperity from the Ascended Host to each one of you, that Its Radiation may go forth to all mankind.

## THE DISCOURSE

One of the important things for all mankind to remember, and especially Students, is to make themselves permanently adamant against all outer suggestion. There is prevalent in the atmosphere the suggestion of things that disturb; and when Students become more sensitive, they must establish a permanent guard against suggestion from the outer, wherever they are.

*A helpful Affirmation:* "*I, my Christ Self, the 'Mighty I AM Presence,' forbid every atom of my outer mind and body to accept anything from anywhere that is less than all of God. I, my Christ Self, the 'Mighty I AM Presence,' command you to receive and permanently record the Eternal Activity of my full Illumination and Freedom on all planes.*"

Whenever one is excited, the door is open. The correct attitude is to constantly declare that there is only the Presence of God acting in and about oneself. A powerful protecting Affirmation is: "*The Mighty Ascended Jesus Christ in me, which is God's Perfection acting, is my Protection, my Defense, and my Deliverance from everything that is undesirable.*" Whenever one is out of God's Harmony, the *inner motion* is started that may flow forth hours or days later, and the individual be quite unaware of what started such a result.

Mankind must understand that each one alone is the cause of all in his or her Life and world. Nothing opens the door so easily and quickly as resentment or irritation. So often one misunderstands expressions used, thereby setting up entirely unnecessary crosscurrents. Whenever one wants understanding, always use, "*There is only God's Perfect Mind in me.*" There is no excuse for heated words or discussions in trying to gain understanding. Obedience is one of the essential things in Life. If we are not obedient to the lesser, then we cannot obey the greater. Love is the most wonderful thing in the World and is the Power of the Universe!

*Unusual weather conditions:* This has not been explained before: Whenever there is a bursting forth through volcanic action, as there has been and as there will continue to be during the summer, there are released interior forces of the Earth; and the sediment that is carried for not only hundreds but thousands of miles, many times brings a complete change of atmospheric conditions. It often causes the heat to be more intense or has the opposite effect of cooling off, depending upon the substance that is released. Just as a cataclysmic condition may change the course of the Gulf Stream and thus the climate, so these forces released in the air cause the atmosphere or climatic conditions to change.

*Encouragement:* For the encouragement of yourselves and the Students, I wish to say with Great Joy in My Heart, that beautiful and wonderful progress is being made by the sincere Students; and because much of that wonderful achievement is not yet in evidence in the outer, should not in anywise be discouraging, for I assure you the growth within each one is remarkable.

*To Mrs. Ballard:* Your power to focus the Love Ray is beautiful indeed. It is one of the most needed things in the World today, and is one of the most important channels through which Justice acts. The Nature of Divine Love is gently positive; but wherever there is a condition requiring it, one may qualify It with greater positiveness or make It dynamically positive—for instance, to dissolve opposition to a higher achievement.

Next week I will be with you in both Classes in person for definite work that needs to be done. Cha Ara and Nada have naturally a great Healing Radiation, and through Their Work it has grown to a Great Intensity. They have contacted that which requires a great deal of Healing Power.

*Important for the home:* Take a very definite stand that nothing comes into your home but the Mighty Christ Presence, which is permanently established there so that all who enter are bound by Divine Love to act in perfect cooperation with everything in the home. Know that everyone who enters your door is caught in the Mighty Embrace of God and is held there forever. Let it become a permanent consciousness, and it will make possible a definite work to be done for the individuals who enter.

*A dynamic shattering Decree:* "Now, 'Mighty

*I AM Presence,' shatter and consume this! See that it does not touch my Life or world again!"* Sometimes a quick dynamic Decree is much more effective than a longer treatment. Remember this: to say to the "Beloved Mighty I AM Presence," *"Shatter and consume this,"* is to shatter the focus of the discord; and the consuming is then easier.

The "Mighty I AM Presence" dwells within the White Fire Body which is a Condensation of Light.

You are always the one who must make the picture and impress it on the within, and the "Presence" within brings forth the manifestation. Shortly, whenever you make pictures they will outpicture very quickly. Feel that when you do a thing, it is God doing it; and it must therefore come forth.

# DISCOURSE VII

*July 25, 1932*

Saint Germain

*INVOCATION:* Thou Mighty Infinite, Governing, Unconquerable "Presence," Thou Mighty God of the Universe, individualized in mankind, we recognize and accept Thy Mighty "Presence," Thy full Power and Activity in our minds and bodies.

We command the outer self to conform in union with Thy Mighty Presence. We command all outer activity to be silent and obey Thy Mighty Behest. We give praise and thanks that Thou art the Only Intelligence ever acting, and that Thy Mighty Energy pours through these outer selves so that they are always self-sustained — that Thou art the Magic "Presence" causing Miracles to manifest and be sustained each day. We give praise and thanks that this is ever so, Eternally.

## THE DISCOURSE

My Love and the Love of the Ascended Host flood your being with Joy, Peace, Confidence, and Perfect

Operation in all things. I am deeply grateful for your lovely cooperation.

The seeming mysteries of Life are so simple and so easily applied once the True Foundation is established in the consciousness. I assure you no one can proceed far on the Pathway until there is a definite Anchorage in the consciousness. There must be no uncertainty.

*The dweller on the threshold:* The simple, entire Truth of the situation is that the dweller on the threshold is an accumulation of the misdirected energy of the Solar Force, which is God's Energy. It is nothing in the world to be feared, but rather there is reason for rejoicing that at last the Truth is forthcoming, in order to dissipate so much fear and misconception of a thing that is very simple. Again, the so-called beast of Biblical description, also understood and described otherwise, is but the misdirection of this Solar Energy — that has been directed downward instead of upward.

This will explain to you the very great importance of the control of the thought; for wherever the attention is directed, the energy is bound to go. Therefore, if you permit the thought or consciousness of anger, resentment, jealousy, or the dissipation of the energy through the thought of sex, you are but turning that Mighty Current downward.

*Free Will:* The Power of Free Will is mankind's great privilege of holding the attention of the consciousness fixed on the Divine "Presence" or Principle of Activity that at all times compels the upward flow of the Mighty Solar Energy. This shows you how simple the process is — at the same time, the necessity of consciously keeping that Energy flowing upward. Therefore, the moment any thought enters the mind that is not in harmony with that idea, take the same attitude you would to a disobedient child who is too young to understand the Laws and say: " *'I AM' Master of my own thought! 'I AM' Master and I direct the Energy where I wish it to go!"* Anyone who will do this, will find that it will give them easy command and regulation of this Energy in a very short time.

*For the home:* No matter what the seeming provocation is, shut out resentment, criticism, condemnation, or anything else that is not in harmony with that Law.

*Remember this forever: You never deal with persons.* The truth is that *you are always dealing with a force* which you must control before you go much farther. Without this control you cannot go beyond a certain point, because in an unguarded moment you would loose forces that would impair your further progress in this embodiment.

Each one should train himself to always hold himself within his own Magic Circle of the Flame of Divine Love, which he has to build around himself consciously. Speak to each other within this Circle; for no matter where you are, the Magic Circle is there. Whenever anyone fixes the attention on that Mighty Presence of God, he is making a Magic Circle, wherein are performed mighty seeming Miracles. This Magic Circle is ever widening and extending, according to the sincerity and intensity with which the attention is held upon that Mighty "Presence."

At first, I assure you, it does require sincere, earnest guard; but if you should slip once in a while, do not let it bother you in any sense. Come right back with still greater unyielding sincerity and intensity. The mistake of a great many Students is that if they are off guard once in a while, they become discouraged—which is childish and foolish. It is of very great value in disciplining ourselves to always remember that every time something occurs which would make us desire to strike back physically or in speech or thought—or cause us to do it—to take this attitude: *"This is but a force to be handled, and these personalities are but an opportunity for me to learn how to control this energy."* This takes away the resistance that starts the activity of the discord which seeks to intrude. As you keep up the conscious guard, you will be surprised how the Magic Circle around you will expand until everyone who contacts you, will love and worship you. Such is the Magic Power of Love and Harmony.

Some of these things may seem simple, but unifying them is the One Great Law. As you begin to think of the Magic Circle, you begin to see and feel It around you; and the more you do this, the more rapidly It builds and expands.

*Negative old habits:* The strange thing is that, from old habit, people allow the attention to enter into the negative conditions; and the first thing they know they are in trouble. In such conditions the Conscious Demand should be, *"Here! thou outer activity! Be silent before the God in me!"* The only activity to be concerned with, is the governing and qualifying of the energy in the outer activity.

When you do anything for the protection of another, there must be some permanent uplift directed to the individual, or it is not permissible for you to do it. Without this, it is a useless direction of energy; and then we do not have the right to use the energy even for the protection. The return of the energy to our own Magnificent Flame of Almighty God is much more rapid than the downward direction of it, and the ratio is about ten to one.

*The intelligent Beings of the four Elements:* Mortals little realize how the intelligent Beings of the four Elements are used for their benefit; indeed most individuals and many Students are inclined to deny Their very existence. Everything that is visible to the outer senses is but a passing picture of the outer creation. Back of the outer creation and within this Great God Energy is the Mighty Reality, which is always visible to the Inner Sight. If Students would say to this Mighty "Presence," *"God! let me see with Thine Eyes—my Inner Sight,"* and follow this by, *"I give thanks I do see now and forever"*—this would many times enable the individual to quickly enter into the Inner Sight, depending on his or her own Inner Attunement. There has not been and will not be anything given in this Instruction but that which will produce absolutely definite results, if applied with an unwavering consciousness.

When Students reach a point where they can be used, it is said that, "Except ye become as little children, ye shall not enter into the Kingdom of Heaven." Sometimes *We* feel as joyous as little children when We see one reaching out to the Light who can be attuned and used. When individuals reach to the Light with great longing and intensity of desire, it isn't a drop in the bucket compared to the Ascended Masters' Desire for Students to be able to receive so they can be used. We need the Student so much who is attuned, so he or she can be used. There is so much need for Students who can be consciously used in any way by the Great Ones.

*Beloved Mighty Oromasis:* Oromasis, the Prince of Fiery Beings, plays a tremendous part in the Life of the individual when he or she comes to a point of this understanding. He is a Prince of the Salamanders who has become Immortalized. You will be amazed and almost dumbfounded when you learn what actually takes place. In the first place, there must be the connection between the Fire Element and the mortals, because the Fire Element does not become Immortalized except by contact with the mortal.

*Creation by the Ascended Masters:* On the Higher or Spiritual Planes of Activity, all Creation takes place by thought. The thought draws to itself the Universal Substance, producing any desired form according to the quality of the desire or thought. The Ascended Host, in projecting into form the Invisible Substance, do qualify it with whatever Quality They wish to use. If it is to resemble the quality of a jewel, They may produce it in a table: this table can be like one jewel or have a combination of the elements of one or all jewels. However, They do not project things for a bargain counter. The quality of the tables would be in harmony with what the people were accustomed to. When the attention is once given an impulse, it draws from the outer that which is nearest reality.

*The sex activity:* The outer sex activity is a perverted interpretation of an original Perfection and Purity.

*Very important for contemplation:* When you become quiet and get deep, deep into the Silence, say, *"Great Self, speak to me."* The mind cannot conceive anything that is not possible of accomplishment.

*BENEDICTION:* Mighty Radiant, Evolving "Presence" of this Center of Divine Radiation! Draw Thy Magic Circle about this home and all its activities. Pour forth Thy Radiant Love, Light, and Activity—drawing into Its Use, Abundance of Thy Wealth; and give Peace, Joy, Harmony, and Perfection through Its Use and Ministrations. Hold each one within his own individual Magic Circle as he moves in the outer world, giving forth Thy Mighty Everlasting, Self-sustaining Strength, Courage, and Consciousness of Thy Directing Presence. Let each one feel himself a Mighty Magnet drawing an Abundance of Wealth for everything he needs, wishes, and desires; and know that the Outpouring is flowing in Its Greatest Abundance.

# DISCOURSE VIII

*July 28, 1932*

SAINT GERMAIN

*INVOCATION:* Thou Mighty Infinite, Radiant One, whose "Mighty I AM Presence" We bow before! Thou Mighty Ruler of the Universe! We bow before Thy All-conquering Power! We accept fully Thy Radiating Presence! We call to Thee, that Thy Presence go before Us everywhere, mastering all conditions We contact and making Us a channel through which Thy Mighty Presence flows.

We bring Love, Greetings, and Blessings to America.

## THE DISCOURSE

Kindness is always the conquering power, both with human beings and animals as well. Out of the fullness of patience and the application of the Presence of Divine Love in all affairs, comes the sure and certain reward. There is no activity where the consciousness or attention is held on the "Mighty I AM Presence," wherein the element of Divine Love is not active; but this natural Activity may be greatly intensified by adding your consciousness of the Quality of Divine Love to it. This is a subtle point which very few, not Ascended, realize.

Some will say, "How is it we mortals may intensify the Activity of God?" I answer: God, the "Mighty I AM Presence," acts through the Free Will of the individual according to his or her acceptance; and the individual, being a part of God, being the same in Quality, has the right and power to increase and intensify *any one* of the natural Activities of God, upon which the consciousness is focused. If sincere Students will meditate on this particular activity, they are certain to receive much benefit.

When the consciousness of the Student is held unwaveringly on the highest center, which is humanly termed the pineal gland and pituitary body, he is recognizing and inviting the Currents, the Rays of Light and Love, from the Electronic Body of his own "Mighty I AM Presence," and also the Assistance of the mighty advanced Individualizations, or Ascended Masters, from that Sphere of Activity.

This may be a shock to some; but as I have intimated before, personalities pray to God, thinking they are being answered by God direct. But I assure you, there are those Messengers who are the Watchers over mankind, who are the dispensers of the

Radiant Currents and who answer all worthy demands. The Messengers from the "Sun behind the Sun," which is the Heart of the Christ Power as we know it today, are the Mighty Messengers who are pressing forward in conducting this Radiance to humanity, in this radiant cycle which has now begun.

In your department stores and schools, there are heads of departments and teachers. This very grossly symbolizes the higher Activity; for in all activity where the Light is coming forth, the less advanced are *always* being taught by the higher. Even the Ascended Host as you know Them, have Those far in advance of Themselves who are Their Instructors. This goes on infinitely and is an important thing for the Student to understand.

I assure you that through the centuries I have never changed in the mode of giving forth the fundamental Principles. To do so would be to cross currents, which would bring disaster instead of the good that I, in My humble Way, have been able to do.

*The most vital thing in human activity is the necessity of positively refusing to sit in judgment on the activity of another human being.* To condemn, criticize, or feel curiosity about the affairs of another, except to wish them Godspeed and that all is well, is not permissible for the real Student or the one who sincerely wishes to reach the highest attainment.

Students and individuals should always remember that there is naught to say them nay in whatever they wish to do or persist in doing—for they have the right to and free use of this Mighty Energy of God, which is the Principle of Life animating them. They may use this energy as they choose, until their experience causes them to face about and turn to the Light of their own volition.

At this point or conclusion, they may receive Great Assistance from Those who are more advanced than themselves, which oftentimes strengthens and enables them to hold fast to the Light. Otherwise at this point they might not have been able of themselves to do so. Thus you can see how very important it is for the Student to understand and fully accept the Presence and Help of God's Messengers of Light.

*Spiritualism:* In order that the Students may not misunderstand this, I wish here to assure you that this has not the slightest thing to do with so-called spiritualism, as outwardly understood today. The Ascended Being who has attained to limitless Heights of Understanding through His own conscious Effort, is as far in advance of the average individual who through his lack of understanding has cast off the physical body, as Light is in advance of darkness.

One of the great stumbling blocks in the way of many earnest Students is the inclination to go to mediums, instead of looking to the "Mighty I AM Presence," the All-wise God above, within, and around themselves. Visiting mediums is not permissible to the sincere Student, because it again means that he is dividing his own allegiance; for the Mighty God within us — *the One and Only God* — commands, *"There shall be no other Gods before Me!" Whatever your attention is upon is your God, for there your energy is flowing, and your energy is your Life!*

*To Donald Ballard:* Your love is like a mantle of fragrance to Me. The love from each one of you has a different fragrance. The embracing presence today is very wonderful.

*The Love Ray:* Divine Love is the Mightiest Presence and Power in the Universe; and when one learns to pour It into every condition less than Itself, he will come to know that he is focusing the core of that Mighty Ray into Its Invincible outer Activity. This Ray of which I speak is the one which has Its own natural Quality of Impenetrability.

*To make yourself absolutely Invincible:* Whenever there comes the idea of disturbance of any kind, no matter what the cause, it is your province as a

Student of the Light to take your unyielding stand, *"There is only God acting in that person, place, or condition!"* Thus you are giving power where it truly belongs; and so, you allow the full Inner Power of the Current of Divine Love to flow. To constantly practice this with joy and certain recognition of your Inner Power of the "Mighty I AM Presence," will make you absolutely Invincible!

Students often say in their Application of the Law, "Oh, it didn't work." I say to you that it is absolutely impossible for it *not* to work, unless in some manner you have given power to the outer appearance.

The unfortunate thing with Students is, sometimes, the failure to notice the small manifestations of that Great "Presence." As we are ever moving from the smaller to the greater, how can we receive the greater if we are not giving recognition to the smaller? I assure you, all of God's Activity moves forward in a perfectly logical manner. The more recognition we give to the small manifestations, the quicker will we receive the greater. For instance in the outer world of education, if the child did not learn its letters and how to combine them, how would it ever in the world become able to form words?

There is a quality within the personal self that sometimes causes it to want to pass over the smaller things as of no value and, to use a modern phrase, "grab off the greater." However, there is not the slightest difference in the Activity of the Mighty Law, whether it be great or small in Its accomplishment, if the Student is sufficiently aware of the "Mighty I AM Presence" acting.

The Student who needs, or thinks he does, some manifestation of the "Presence" to give him faith in accomplishing the greater, will find great benefit in meditating upon this humble endeavor to make clear the way. *The moment a demand for a thing comes, it shows that it is forthcoming!*

*Raising the body:* We first raise the body in consciousness. When we become conscious that *it is possible for us to raise the body*, and take the determined stand to do it—that moment the Law of our being is set into motion to produce the perfected accomplishment.

I assure you that the Mighty Law, when given a chance through your outer volition, loses no time in utilizing the opportunity, unless at some time you change about and cease to recognize this as a certain accomplishment. If you maintain this determination, you will find at some future time that the force set in motion in the beginning for that purpose, never ceased for one moment to work for that end.

If we do not utilize the Knowledge that God has

already given, how can we expect to have more? This Instruction and Information is not given just to hear oneself talk, but is *Ascended Master Law and Information placed at the disposal of the Students;* and if they will look to their Master Selves, the "Mighty I AM Presence," for direction, they will be caused to use the right Application at the right time for the right thing required.

I say this: that where a great deal of Information and Application is given within a certain time, there is much given so the Student may select that which he or she needs at a specific time for a specific purpose. If I allowed you to look to Me, the Instruction would defeat Its own purpose. Never in the history of the World has there been a time when so much Instruction and Information has been given, for *the Incoming Cosmic Christ is now in command.* Never has there been such Application and Assistance given to Students; for the Cosmic Outpouring is omnipresent, helping the Student who will give his or her attention.

*Beloved Surya:* Surya is a Place as well as an Individuality. It is the Name of one of the Individualized Activities of the Great Central Sun. It is impossible not to receive what comes from the "Mighty I AM Presence" as an idea, when you really know that it is God sending or giving the idea.

*Affirm often:* "It is impossible for anything to happen anywhere in my Life but God's Perfect Activity."

*Note:* When you give power to astrology, you are putting dynamite in your own pathway.

*BENEDICTION:* "Mighty I AM Presence" from the Great Central Sun! We give praise and thanks for Thy Mighty Outpouring this day, for Thy Eternal Victory of Divine Love that in Its Glorious Majesty holds Dominion — *now* — throughout mankind and the Earth. We glorify Thee forever, Thou "Mighty I AM Presence"!

(Reprinted from September 1936 *Voice of the "I AM"*)

# DISCOURSE IX

*August 1, 1932*

SAINT GERMAIN

*INVOCATION:* Thou most Infinite, Radiant One, Thou who dost possess all Peace, Power, and Wisdom, We give praise and thanks for Thy Holy Presence with Us.

## THE DISCOURSE

*The Cherubim:* We have a very delightful Manifestation of the Great Presence here today. A Cherubim from One of the Seven Elohim is sent to dispense Its Radiance; and It enfolds the room in a Ray of Golden Light, touched with a Breath of Pink. This Presence rests at anchor, as it were, about sixty feet above the home; and from It extends the Golden Ray enfolded in Its Garment of Love.

The Cherubim are similar to the Angel Devas, but nearer the human size. Sometimes the Cherubim are quite like the well-rounded form of a small lady. They always convey Love as the predominating Quality or Activity. The Angel Devas often convey

71

the element of Power because of the Work They have to do. The Cherubim have such a Mighty Focus of the Love Ray that They accomplish whatever They wish through It. They have a great Radiance for a great distance.

*The Cherubim's Message:* "Beloved Ones, chosen of the Light, We add Our Love with this Enfolding Radiance to strengthen, to heal, to bless, and to prosper each one of you, and to cleanse every particle of thought of self away, so that the Full Presence of the Christ may have Its Dominion of Full Peace, Love, and Harmony within the body, that it may have perfect health."

This Presence gives Its Love and Greetings to each one, so that they may feel Its Presence henceforth, enfolding and unfolding in each one. In this Ray is a Special Ray to each one of you, that will henceforth remain anchored in the Heart to fulfill Its Mission. The Presence of the Cherubim wishes me to say that you may think of It as "The Presence of the Golden Heart."

*The spinal Currents:* Today, We will take up an Explanation that, as far as I know, has not heretofore been given. The Currents of the Negative and Positive Force, one on either side of the spine, ever active in Their mission of distribution, are like two harp strings: the Negative being of the bass, and the

Positive of the treble. There is within the nerve on each side of the spine, that which resembles a harp string. When one enters the Conscious Path, these Divine Strings, as it were, begin to be tuned; and when they reach a certain tautness, they begin to respond to the Great Advanced Presences who play upon them, unknown to the human form.

When the human form sometimes feels a tension, it is because some discordant vibration has touched one of these Strings. There is perfected a tiny Instrument that, when placed at the base of the brain, acts like a key to the harp, attuning these Strings to the proper Activity. It is under consideration now whether this shall be brought forth. If it be brought forth, certain ones who may receive It are to be prepared for the Intense Use of the Cosmic Rays. This accounts for the special Presence with us today.

*Warning:* I ask each one of you to take a firm grip on yourself, putting out of the mind everything of a discordant nature, especially during the month of August and possibly September. The one who succeeds in doing this will receive great benefit. The one who will govern his thought, shutting out all discord, will open himself to the Mighty Current that will attune the Harp Strings of the Soul, just described. Through these one may receive distinct Hearing of the Inner "Presence," and clear Vision beyond the Veil.

Just be at peace, ease, and rest concerning these; feel no strain in any way, no anxiety. This will give one the Jewel of Inner Discrimination, which will enable him to completely govern the outer activity. This means that it will enable one to distinguish between the human and the Divine Thought, and to govern the outer so that any thought of jealousy, resentment, or self-pity cannot enter. Those three conditions are most stifling to the Higher Activity.

*Visualizing the Harp Strings of the Soul:* I would suggest—the individual should follow his or her feelings—that those who can, visualize these two Harp Strings of the Soul connected at the base of the spine, connecting again at the pineal gland in the brain: the one on the right side of a delightful Pink and the one on the left side an intense Blue. The Pink conveys Powerful Divine Love through the Positive Current; and the Blue String, the Negative Current, sustains the outer form in the Divine Balance. This description given, I assure you, is very real— quite as real as your harp before you when you sit down to play. The Knowledge of this and Its use, that is and will be given, will enable one to consciously hold a steady, calm balance in the outer contemplation of the Inner "Presence."

In Our—the Great Ones'—Activity at a given time of action, as so ably illustrated at the close of *The*

*Magic Presence*, We often find the Great Wisdom from the still Higher Spheres completing an Action that We might hesitate to do. In that instance and the instance today, it shows the Presence and Activity of a very Great Wisdom that will not allow the outer to interrupt the progress. The time has come for definite, mighty Action.

The song, "Onward Christian Soldiers," sends forth an Activity which is really "Onward Children of the Light." I expect that this Presence may inspire you with the Melody of the "Children of the Light"; for it is really the March of the Eternal Host onward to the Victory of Justice and Eternal Harmony, manifest in the outer expression of humanity.

The Presence which has been established is in answer to the Call to Surya. The Province of this Presence will be to watch and aid in the governing of these two Currents of Attunement.

*Healing:* Beloved Cyclopea is in charge of the Healing Ray to the Earth. The Healing Ray, which is a blending of Gold and Violet, is always an Independent Ray. The Gold is Divine Love, and the Violet is Spiritual Power and the Consuming Activity which dissolves human accumulation.

For Peace, the Gold is predominant. For Spiritual Power as the Consuming Activity, the Violet will predominate. The Violet Ray is a calm, quiet Power and is always an Uplifting Presence. The Blue Ray is Power unqualified. *Always be sure—be careful* not to send your own conscious power with It or to taint It with a feeling of anger or irritation when you use It.

The means described is the Way by which the Ascended Masters often give Great Assistance to the Students, when they put aside, or out of the consciousness, all thought or feeling of self. When one has the complete action of It grasped in the outer mind, It becomes a Mighty Means of Healing.

You will very readily have the use of this; and if you use It for Healing, no matter what seems to be there, hold the two colors positive and steady. *There is no Healing to be done except in the outer form, but be sure to keep the Inner "Presence" at work healing the wounds of hate.* Ask the "Mighty I AM Presence" of the other individual to illumine his or her Heart and mind and then heal the body. All Healing is but a bringing back of a Natural Balance of the two Forces. You will at once see what a Mighty Power you have in your hands to use.

*Note: the celebration of the Crystal Stone:* After seeing the celebration of the Crystal Stone, the scene was a fragment of a past experience; and if it could be dramatized in pictures it would be of immense help to humanity. In spite of all that may seem to be, that wonderful phase of expression, the movies, which can be made so perfectly wonderful, will yet be used to convey Mighty Inner Truths of the Activity of the Mighty Ascended Host. The scene was of a forgotten period of which the only records are in the Royal Teton.

A Mighty Inner Preparation has been made sometime, somewhere, for this outer experience. The Inner Activity is the Real and the only Real, Natural Activity. The outer is so crude and distorted compared to the Inner.

*The situation in Washington, D.C.:* The only right attitude for every Student towards every apparent manifestation of the outer during this seemingly chaotic period is this: No matter what seems to be taking place, drive into the midst of whatever the condition may be, the Consciousness that there is but One Cause that has any Power — and that is the Wisdom, Power, and Presence of Almighty God in Full Action there. Sometimes the outer activity must reach a certain peak of expression to burn out, as it were, the human generation of wrong action. We must know positively and with certainty, that back of every outer activity are God and His Messengers watching the moment to strike, and pouring into the condition that Presence which consumes the wrong and raises the Right into its Perfect Activity.

Thus throughout the ages, have God and His Noble Messengers watched the inhumanity to mankind—at each opportunity raising them a little higher, until the Cosmic Signal sounded, foretelling the Onrush of the Mighty Active Presence of Christ, *God in Action*, that will draw the poisonous fangs from the poor serpent of mankind—so that willingly its forces are forever turned upward. The serpent will then have become the Dove, for the serpent was first conceived in the mind of the outer man by the misdirection of that wonderful Energy of God. It was thus turned downward from Its Rightful Heavenly course—which is forever upward.

Do not at any time feel disturbance at any of the things that take place in the outer world, for all is tending upward towards its Eternal Perfection. Woe unto those in official places who fail to act in accordance with those strong Inner Promptings that they are receiving clearly and distinctly, for many are receiving them unmistakably. President Hoover felt that there were important records and much that needed to be protected; and he knew that when a crowd gets into a mob vibration, they do things which they never intended in the beginning. He was right, for violence would have become rampant. If the veterans had had a little more encouragement in their intent, they would have burned and destroyed things which needed to be preserved. [This refers to the veterans' march on Washington, D.C., July 1932. This was a time of great economic depression.] During the time of the French Revolution, Robespierre had no idea in the beginning that things would go as far as they did.

*The attitude of the real Student: "There is only God acting in this situation, and He will bring Right and Justice out of it!"*

When people will not listen, they must go on until you knock them for a "home run" before they will pay attention. Awake! and stand for the One Presence of Right and Justice! The willingness to face the human creation and its error, and turn about, takes very great strength.

*Vital:* Thought gets to revolving, stirring up, and generating the feeling; then it becomes difficult to control it. To any disturbing thought say, *"I refuse to let you act—now get out!"* Every Student should face himself, see what there is that needs correcting, and then proceed to correct it. There is only one cause in every individual's Life, and that is his own conscious creation. Every Student has to get that idea into his head, face it, and then conquer himself. Instead of recognizing God as the only Cause, the mass of mankind generate, through the outer manifestation, misconceptions and causes that are certain to bring them distress.

The idea of the dragon was first a conception in the ancient Chinese civilization. At that time the wrong use of the Solar Force created, instead of a thought-form resembling the human, a thought-form resembling the serpent, because they had for generations been taught and had known the Creative Power as the serpent power—which caused the thought creation to take that form. That tradition has come down with the Chinese to the present day, as you will observe in their ceremony of the New Year. They masquerade as the dragon to scare away the evil spirits. This is but a distorted conception of the Great Wisdom that they once used.

*Discourses:* The arrangements for the days on which these Discourses are given have been quite wisely planned. While the Instruction is going forth, this makes it possible to carry the Radiation from lesson to lesson, and is better for the Class and gives the Radiation intended for them.

*For the young Students:* The time has arrived when a special effort will be made to reach those from twelve years on, with the Understanding of the Light. There are many Great Souls who have come into embodiment since the war period; and once the contact is made, they will instantly feel the Inner Response. Whoever feels that Response will receive great benefit from the outer contact with the Truth.

*Important daily:* It is wise to always keep using the Command: *"I, Christ, the 'Mighty I AM Presence,' command that there be no interference in the Truth being conveyed to anyone, for Truth is always Its own Defense."* This will cause to be projected about the younger Students a Presence that will not accept suggestions that might lead them away from the Truth and from the "Presence"—from which they felt the Inner Response.

Just declaring a thing often enables it to be done. It is hard for Students to conceive that a certain, positive declaration often opens wide the door to the enlargement of the demand, as it were. It is so easy for the Student always to govern thought if he or she will only do it before it gains momentum. Say: *"Here! Now, stop! Get out!"* The thing the outer self needs is unshakable confidence; because it has not been accustomed to Instantaneous Manifestation, it feels things are far off, so to speak.

*Don's grown appearance:* If Don loves Me and occasionally looks at My picture, he might easily take on a resemblance. Nada has an amazing Power through the use of the Love Ray.

*Our new Home:* The establishment of an Ascended Master Home is entirely within the province of that Intelligence that comes forth at intervals.

The best way is just to rejoice in the idea and let the Great Wisdom bring it about. Many times it is absolutely essential that the idea be conveyed to the outer; for through that, certain preparation can be made which saves a great deal of energy.

*BENEDICTION:* Thou Great Glorious, Radiant "Presence"! Thou who art the Wisdom, Power, and Love—the Inflow of Light enfolding each one! Mighty God of Light! Thou Mighty Eternal, Radiant One art forever the Governing Presence of these Thy Children!

# DISCOURSE X

*August 4, 1932*

SAINT GERMAIN

*INVOCATION:* Thou Mighty Infinite, Majestic "Presence"! We give praise and thanks for the Outpouring of Thy Mighty Messengers. This day when Thou hast sent forth Thy Mighty Messengers to bless America, We are cognizant of Thy Mighty Activity —Thou Mighty God, the One, the Supreme—unfolding Truth through Thy Wondrous Individualization that every hour, every day, is drawing nearer the Perfection of Truth in the outer activity.

In the Heart of each is the Cosmic Perfection taking place. To all who look to Truth, as a Mighty River comes the Outpouring from Thee.

## THE DISCOURSE

For the first time in five thousand years, there is being sent forth an Outpouring of this kind to America. There are Seven Sun-Centers in America to which Seven Great Beings are this day pouring out a Mighty Radiance. Four of these places are New

York, Chicago, Denver, and Seattle. The Seven Great Ones at this time are Cosmically permitted to intensify the Mighty Christ Presence that is steadily moving forward into the consciousness of humanity.

At two o'clock this morning, seven Pathways of Light might have been seen in the sky. This portends much for the Blessing of America, in fact for the entire North America. These Great Beings whose attention has been called to this sincere Channel that has made the point of the wedge through which They have found entrance, whereby They may shed Their Light into the darkened spots of human civilization—They send you a Wondrous Message: the Promise that you shall have Great and Powerful Use of the Light Rays.

*The Cherubim and Its Message:* The Beloved Cherubim is enthroned, holding Its Conscious Radiance about you today. The Loving Message to you is this: "Fear not what any mortal may do; command silence of the outer in the Name of that Ascended 'Presence,' and all the outer must bow the knee before that Mighty 'Presence' and be at Peace." Again come the Words from over the ethers: "Thou shalt yet know, feel, see, and experience what Loyalty to the Light and the Ascended Host means."

No matter what any mortal may seem to manifest, hold fast always to the fact that the Omnipresent,

Mighty God and His Chosen Messengers govern the Earth and its inhabitants in spite of any seeming appearance to the contrary. The God of Light, Love, Wisdom, and Power is anchored within your lives, within your world, and is the Conquering, Silencing, Supplying, Invincible Presence and Power. Know this and be at peace.

*To Mrs. Ballard:* Again, may I express to you My Appreciation for the attention given to the National Anthem; for it has given Me an opportunity to do for America, the Jewel of My Heart, that which I have not had the opportunity to do since the signing of the Declaration of Independence. Others have their times of rejoicing; today is My turn. As We never fail to give praise and thanks for the smallest Manifestation of that Mighty Invincible "Presence," so in proportion to that Mighty Power of a Manifestation do We, in Intensified Consciousness, give forth gratitude and praise. So you see We are no different from yourselves; for no matter what the Height attained, We are always ready to put self aside and give praise and thanks for the opportunity to consume and dissolve anything that would impede that Mighty Onward Progress.

Always keep before the Student the fact that self-pity is one of the most stifling things which impede individual progress, and yet it is so easily governed when once understood. Every Student of the Light should, at least once a day, take inventory of his consciousness and see wherein there is an element that needs eliminating, and then proceed to do it. This must be done by the use of the Consuming Flame. In this way, he keeps the consciousness cleared and the pathway open to the Mighty Inspiration, and he will be much less annoyed and disturbed by undesirable thoughts.

*The Three Plumes of the Soul:* Out of the Great Glory of the Conquering of the outer self, is the Soul crowned with the Three Plumes of Sustaining Power. These Plumes, I assure you, are Real and Tangible. This Good Brother is the only one who has described Them outside of the Arisen Host, as you will find in the second visit to the Royal Teton in the manuscript [*Unveiled Mysteries*]. The Three Plumes of Light proceeding from the Globe of Light never leave those who have reached a certain Attainment, and may be seen by all who use the Inner Sight. At first It is a blended, soft Light; but It grows in Strength as the Consciousness is held on this Highest Center within the individual. It steadily increases until It forms three small Plumes no larger than your finger. It continues to increase until They reach three feet. In form They are almost identical to the most beautiful ostrich plumes one could imagine. At one time in the history of England, the symbolism of the Three Plumes of the Prince of Wales was known, and also in France; but it is now forgotten.

A most remarkable Manifestation of the Mighty Inner Power has recently taken place. Heretofore — in fact for many centuries — worded expressions have had to be clothed, or shall I say Divine Expressions had to be clothed, so that only the worthy might be able to interpret Their Inner Meaning. Many of these Great Inner Expressions will be laid bare to the observations of mankind, to give them an opportunity of utilizing this Wisdom — if they only will. If there is not within the Soul-advancement of the individual that which recognizes the uncovering of this Divine Expression, then he or she will pass it by; but if there be one or many that recognize the Truth, then to those will Great Assistance be given.

*How the Student may help in national activity:* You can give Me great assistance in national activity if you will make it a point whenever you read a negative report, to instantly take the conscious stand that there is only God and His Perfection there, sustained by His Mighty Messengers. It would be well if the Student should have this especially. This will do much to transmute and change the expression of the press. Whenever you see a negative expression by the press, command all the press to be God's Messengers of Right and Truth—for ere long, it will not be a shield or puppet in the hands of politicians.

There will be placed a Mighty Messenger to control or govern the press; and when the change begins to tangibly take place, the members of the press will be amazed many times at their own audacity in expressing the Truth, where in the past they expressed falsehood. So you will see that God's Mighty Command has in nowise waxed short, but rather challenges mankind: *"Try Me and see if I will not pour out a Blessing, that there will not be room to receive It."* Often give the Command, *"Let there be Light!"*

*Very important:* I would suggest that you read that Message every other day so that it keeps these promises before you. A certain sort of Exaltation of the Soul goes forth through the recognition of It.

In times past the Student was not given any encouragement at all until he came to a certain point. So today, the Student is very fortunate. In times past, the Strength of the Student had to be proven. It is proven today in a way just as powerful, but unknown to the Student. He is taking his Initiation in the outer world. He is being made bulletproof, for now he is building his own Armor, a Permanent, Eternal thing.

Again, I feel I must say how really fortunate the Student is today in having the Assistance of the

Mighty Cosmic Christ. It seems to Me that when the Student really learns this, he will exert everything within his power to harmonize himself within himself, because he knows he has the Assistance of this Mighty Cosmic Presence.

Lest I might be misunderstood, the reason I speak especially of America today is because, as We have said before, America is the homecoming of the white race. Naturally, at such a homecoming, there must be prepared a great Feast of Light. It really is not possible to convey in words just what an individual Recognition and Acceptance of a Presence or Activity sometimes mean.

It is so difficult for the average Student to realize that he can be an Unlimited Channel for the Outpouring of these Great Messengers. When one becomes aware that he can be such a Channel for Outpouring, he should put aside all inharmonious thought within, or that which approaches him from without, as he would a poisonous serpent. When the outer self sees that it has lost its foothold and is slipping into oblivion, it concocts all kinds of pretenses to try to gain recognition; but when the firm determination is there to think, feel, and experience only the Beauties of the Christ, then there is left no opening for the outer to intrude itself and cause disturbance.

It is very great Law that when a friend voluntarily

wishes to give Assistance in holding another in the Light, he or she may do what even the teacher may not be permitted to do. So you see that your Impelling Power has been wise indeed. A Master may not go beyond certain limits with His Students; hence He wishes you to have this unusual explanation. *Therefore, every real Student will always withhold all criticism, no matter what the appearance may be.* People are so prone to sit in judgment on others, seeing only appearances and letting the criticism run rampant, no matter what the Truth.

The Point of Light within is the Brain of the Electron. It seems very strange that Students have not realized that the Spirit of Mentality acts on the physical body. If there were no Life, Substance, Truth, or Intelligence in matter, how could it be acted upon, as they have seen many times? For Intelligence to act, there must be Intelligence to be acted upon.

*To Mrs. Ballard:* It will be a Glorious Celebration when you reach the Full Accomplishment of knowing where you have been, are going, and what you have received.

A remarkable expression I loved to use and I often contemplate today, is, *"The matter of knowing God is simply the restoration of forgotten memory."* We have known God before because we are God-created. When we began the descent into dense activity, we had the complete conscious memory. When the energy was directed downward, the veil was drawn; and the Marvelous, Glorious Beauty of that Wondrous Temple of God was forgotten. Now, that forgotten memory is steadily and surely being brought again into the conscious, outer activity. The amazing thing is that so few seem to have fallen into the idea that anyone with persistent effort could command that *that complete Divine Memory be restored* — and it would be done. Few have had the patience to continue long enough to get sufficient encouragement to go on. Give the Command that the full Divine Memory be restored — and It will be manifest shortly.

*The use of the hands in speech: Don asked,* "Why does Mama talk with her hands?"

*Answer:* Few can see what takes place with the person who uses intense movement of the hands in discoursing or explaining. A certain amount of energy is liberated, but not wasted. Many times where specific information is being given, the energy liberated in that manner helps the person to whom the explanation is being given, to receive it.

If you will notice, there are times when the hands are not used, and again there are times when they are used in almost violent action. If Billy Sunday, and others of like strenuosity, could have known what they could have accomplished by beating the table with the open instead of the closed hands, they would have added greatly to their conversions. The hand is an outlet of the energy; consequently, those who from former knowledge possess great strength, are usually powerful in lifting and handling great weights. The energy always goes where it is directed.

*The Vestal Virgins in the ancient temples:* There was a time when the Vestal Virgin was given Tremendous Power to draw into Manifestation the Mighty Presence—the Activity of the Ray as the Flame. That was why in the beginning the Priestess could do what the Priest did not dare attempt, in drawing the Mighty Focus of this Invisible Fire. This was often greatly intensified by the King of the Fire Element, Oromasis. Of course at that time, explanations of those things were not given. Sometimes the Priest saw this Presence and Assistance, but rarely if ever was advised as to who or what the Presence was.

*The Cherubim and Seraphim:* The Cherubim has always been the Special Direct Messenger of God and has always assisted the Seven Great Lords of the Flame from Venus, and also the Elohim. The Seraphim are the next step higher. They are rarely if ever used in the same capacity as the Cherubim. Sometimes the Cherubim manifest as a Sun or a Flame of many colors. It is rarely that They manifest in the human form as we know it.

*BENEDICTION:* Thou Radiating "Presence," as We are held within the Radiance of Thy most Gracious Smile, and the Embrace of Thy Great Self, We offer praise and thanks that Thou hast been sent to bless, to heal, to illumine — and that Thou dost command the Dwellers within the Earth to reveal Their Secrets to these Thy Messengers.

# DISCOURSE XI

*August 8, 1932*

SAINT GERMAIN

*INVOCATION:* Thou Mighty Infinite "Presence," Thou All-Sustaining Power in the Cosmic World and in the Life of the individual. Thou art the only "Presence" and Energy. O Thou Mighty Light, clothe us with Thy Mighty Radiance that We may shine forth like the Great Sun, to heal, to bless, to enlighten all with whom We come in contact, and manifest Thy Mighty Sustaining Power. Silence and bring into subjection the outer self and activity that would spread its shadows in the Presence of the Light.

We take Our stand with firm determination to walk, to live, to be Thy Mighty "Presence" and Light. We give no quarter to the human or outer self that would interfere. We recognize, claim, and accept only Thy Mighty Radiant "Presence," Thy Mighty Sustaining Wisdom and Strength to lead Us forth on Thy Pathway of Life — ever upward and onward, ever sustained by Thy Mighty "Presence" until at last We have attained Thy Gift of Dominion over the outer self and enter into the Temple of Light.

### THE DISCOURSE

*Instruction:* I regret that you have not understood the importance of being in bed by midnight, so that certain Work might go on at those hours. It is important that the body be at rest by midnight. Certain Work is accomplished then; tremendous Work has been planned and cannot go on without the fullest cooperation — and I am sure you are glad to do that.

*Obedience:* In all Activity of Life the highest attainment without obedience may fall to the lowest. In the beginning when the Divine became lowered to the present density, it was through the lack of obedience. Unless you can feel this willing, joyous obedience, it is not possible to continue this Work. We are glad to give Assistance. I will give you Help and Strength to help you obey. It is only because of Love for you that We want you to hold to this condition for the Work. We cannot use any of Our Force to compel.

*Use this every day:* "Today, I will stand guard; and I will not become so interested in the outer activity that it will not give me opportunity to receive the Great Radiance of the 'Presence.' God, govern and sustain me in the governing and mastery of the *outer conditions."*

*Determination and Divine Will:* One of the greatest and mightiest simple Truths is to know that an unyielding determination for any specific accomplishment is the Open Doorway by which the Inner Strength flows out to its accomplishment. In our present era of activity, I think it is very well that Students should understand that what has always been termed "will" by the Instructors, is but determination to hold to the Light and that Eversustaining "Presence."

I have observed so often that, like many other expressions used, the word "will" is not understood. There is only one Will that can be used, and that is the Divine Will. If we take a firm, unyielding determination to accept nothing but the Mighty Presence of God and that Activity of the Light, we are drawing into powerful action the Divine Will. However, I think it is much more readily understood by using this term "determination," for that cannot be misunderstood. This I am sure will help greatly the Students that come under This Radiation. There is only one Energy that can be used, and that is the Life Principle in the individual, which is God's Energy.

*Please understand:* Therefore when individuals aim, through the attention and determination, to use this energy constructively, then they have entered into the fullness of the outer activity that will loose the Inner Activity to do the work. Students so often unknowingly drop into the mental attitude that they of the outer have to do certain things, when the True Activity is but to keep the attention centered upon that Mighty Inner God Power which is the only "Presence" that can ever achieve any permanent results.

*The certain Victory:* The conscious use of Decreeing, backed up by the conscious determination, is an Invincible Power and cannot be interfered with when the determination is held unyielding. Everyone knows what "determination" means, leaving no wavering or questioning in the mind. But to most people the word "will" leaves a peculiar sense of vacancy in the consciousness because of the uncertainty of just what it means in the individual's activity and use. I want this to be very clear and definite, for it is the stumbling block over which many trip.

*The difference between human and Divine Will:* So few, even among Students, can distinguish between what is called the human and the Divine Will. Therefore, We think it much better when referring to the Inner Activity, to use "Divine Will" — and "determination" when referring to the outer activity. This explanation will make it impossible for confusion to accumulate in the mind. Knowing that the outer determination to do or accomplish something, opens the Inner Door for the Inner Power to rush forth to its fulfillment — this removes instantly all uncertainty that it can be done. This is so important to the Student who wishes continuous, definite progress.

In the Retreats, every Student is given private work, particularly in regard to his or her own individual activity. Until now, there has not been given out a clear understanding so the Students could utilize and apply it, except in the Retreats.

In moving in the outer world there can always be this same constant Love and Prayer for your Light and Protection. When you have been in contact with the outer vibration, it takes a very positive force to repel that outer contact and release you from that disturbing element. There may not be the slightest thing noticeable in the outer activity, but sometimes the mere contact with the disturbance of the outer world allows it to rush in if you are not on guard.

This Work must not be interrupted for the gratification of the outer self or activity. Everywhere you go, know and use always, *"God! surround me, and protect me from every outer vibration!"* This is one of the rarest privileges where I have been allowed to warn the Student. Owing to our home life of long ago, it is permitted that I warn you. If this Work is uninterrupted there will come tremendous Light, Abundance, and Freedom; and tremendous things will be accomplished. The reason that I speak of this is that Obedience is the most important of all things. Nothing so destroys the attention as rebellion within; for it not only rebels to the outer but to the Inner.

*For writing:* If you are accustomed to writing, make up your mind before you begin, to keep a certain spot as a focus. If you move, it changes the current and you never get exactly the same condition again. The time has come when the Students must anchor to a definite, perfect thing and hold to it. This Brother years ago took the determined stand to know the Truth and hold to It. All Students should take the same stand to know the Truth absolutely. Then they do not take on a condition they have to get rid of later.

*Foresight:* "*God in me, give me foresight and guard all future activity that all concerning it may be maintained harmoniously.*" "Foresight" means that we are loosing the Inner Protection against any approaching disturbance.

*Divine Memory:* "Divine Memory" covers all speech, thought, and action. "Memory" is that which has accrued from former speech, thought, and action.

*The Guarding Activity of the Cherubim:* Govern

the feeling at all times, for it builds that which even an Ascended Master may not interfere with. A certain sudden concentration upon the Cherubim in the Student's mind, is good now.

Where a reference is made to the Hierarchy of Cherubim, say They are direct Messengers of God. It is a very rare thing when the Cherubim can give direct Radiation, as is done here. There is usually one step down to the point given. We are sustained by our own Mighty God Self within and the Ascended Host or Watchers. The Cherubim is a Dynamo or charging forth of the Power of Divine Love. They are Guardians of Force that has been focused, and of Foci to be. Others work under Them. Sometimes there are two or three steps down, depending on the requirements of the human channels through which They are to operate.

Always feel your own God Self holding you in Its Arms, and know that all is dispelled and you are free.

The Cherubim guard Shamballa, as well as the Great Ones Themselves. The Cherubim guard the Ark of the Covenant. That is the case always when the Manifestation of a High Power comes within a mixed force. Whenever a Being comes like this, you can imagine the importance of the Focus established here. If the Great God saw fit to place a Cherubim as a Guardian over this Focus, you must know it is of great importance. Thus you see how great this can grow in this civilization. As you read about the buried cities of the Amazon in *Unveiled Mysteries*, you will see how such a Focus takes place.

Nothing in the Universe can say nay to an individual if he chooses to turn his vision down. Very few Students get this idea fully. One must of his own volition be joyously willing to render Service to the Light if he is to have help. The Student who sees that he has made mistakes and, through the God within, has the power to consume them, will certainly take the reins and do it—and thus rid himself of barnacles, centuries old.

The fact is that God can consume that which has been personally generated. Anything that has been humanly generated can be dissolved and consumed, because God's Energy was used to create and, when requalified, has the Power to consume and re-create. When an individual says in a half-hearted manner, "It is consumed," it is not necessarily so—unless there was Power or Energy enough released to do it. When one gives a Real Command and means it, the feeling within it always carries force, and that force is its Accomplishing Power.

*Instruction on* Unveiled Mysteries: The Scepter in the hand of the feminine figure in the Tapestry symbolized the focusing of the Eternal Cosmic Power for

the Center in the Royal Teton. The Globe represented the fact that the future Activity of the Retreat
and the Earth was known. The reason why I think
you have the feeling that you should dwell considerably on that Tapestry, is because it would be well to
dwell in detail on the description which reveals that
They were the Founders of the Retreat.

*Question:* "Where are You going today?"

*Saint Germain:* To Arabia, in the Retreat. There
is no time that We meet here that there is not a
Direct Ray sent to Washington for consciously directed Work. We do not have a Focus in Washington
like this, but We do have Messengers there.

*Angel Deva and Cherubim:* Through a consciously
directed focus, the Angel Deva and Cherubim can
pour Their Streams of Force out through the individual's own outgoing Stream.

*Sleep and the Great Great Silence:* "Sleep" is entering the Great Silence. As the outer self becomes
inactive, the Inner Action is released.

*Affirmations:*

Use this constantly: *"I move within the core of the
Ray from the Great Central, Spiritual Sun, and
'I AM' always within Its Invincible Protection!"*

Say to your Mighty Master within: *"Reveal to me
something that will put my finances which are mine
by Divine Right, into my hands quickly; and sustain*

*me in it, through overwhelming and everlasting Light and Love!"* Say also: *"Open Your Channels for my Mighty Supply! Put it in my hands now and continue it permanently!"*

*"God! Open all channels for my money supply now, and I accept nothing else!"* Your only business is with the Master within. Say to It: *"Dispense this in Thy Perfect Way through me in Wisdom and Love!"*

It replies: *"I, Christ, the 'Beloved Mighty I AM,' being declared and to nothing else turning, show thee hidden riches from Secret Places."*

Surrender all attention to the "I AM Presence" within you. Any one of you can now take the Consciousness of a new activity and accomplish it as surely as you live.

Say often, joyously: *"I stand with God, the Supreme, Reigning, Conquering 'I AM Presence'; and as that 'I AM Presence,' I do not want for any good thing!"* Say also: *"God! Give me some money now, today!"* This can no more fail than the Universe can cease to exist.

Know: *"This home is sealed in the Heart of the Cosmic Light and Love, and every right desire is created instantly!"*

Remember forever: *"The moment you fight a thing, it fights you back!"* Always be on guard when the destructive element is discussed or read about.

Live every moment of the day in the Consciousness of the All-powerful Presence of God in you. Say to yourself: *"I have the Mighty Presence of God in me, and I do not give recognition or power to anything else!"* There is nothing that can stand before that Invincible Presence of Almighty God, and all things must be and are compelled to bow before It and obey.

The first thing in the morning, take the determined stand that *"only the Ascended Host of Light can contact me mentally this day!"*

Never fail to use: *"There are no personalities! There is only God in Action at every point! 'I AM' the only 'Presence' acting!"*

Say to your God within: *"My Great Love Self, I do receive instantly all of everything I require!"*

*BENEDICTION:* Thou Mighty "Presence"! We give praise and thanks for Thy Wondrous Radiation and Sustaining Power! All unlike the Christ is consumed; and all now goes forth clothed with the Sustaining Activity of Thy Mighty Presence, holding all within Thy Great Silence and pouring forth Thy Greatest Activity.

# DISCOURSE XII

*August 11, 1932*

SAINT GERMAIN

*INVOCATION:* Thou Mighty Majestic "God Presence"! whose seeming Mystery of Life enfolds Thy Creation, make that "seeming" a Joyous Reality to Thy Children of Earth. Enfold them in Thy Wonderful Radiance, illumining the Pathway of each one that they stumble not. Infinite is Thy Patience! Enduring is Thy Love! Great is Thy Peace! — Thou Wondrous "Presence," active in all mankind. Thou Mighty Presence called "Nature," responding to the God within Thy Creation, pour forth Thy Lavish Abundance upon these Thy Children. Children of the four Elements, I call unto Thee! Come! and minister to the Children of Light! Oh, that each one would keep the Love Radiance burning, that every other condition might be put aside for the inflow of that Mighty "Presence"!

## THE DISCOURSE

Where there is no thought or feeling of rebellion, judgment, or resentment of one another, what Glorious Heights can be reached. Again, I congratulate you on the wonderful condition supplied. The God in each is Master, especially of the mentality. The mentality, if rightly understood, is God's Action. Where God is—*there* is naught else. Say often, *"God alone is here, and I see and feel naught else."* The son is father to the man. The daughter is mother to the woman. Does that sound paradoxical? I assure you it is not; for as a rule the suggestion enfolding the child from five to twelve or fourteen years of age, is that which makes the character of the man or woman unless, through the Conscious Knowledge in practicing the Presence of God, they release and consume all suggestion infringing, and walk forth in the True Inner "Presence."

The unfortunate thing—and in this respect I mean entirely the delay of progress, for there is nothing comes that is not needful—is the lack of knowledge in warding off suggestions that are intruders upon our God-given Freedom. Hence, the reason for the wise statement that our friends are sometimes our worst enemies. *For anyone, outside of a Teacher (I mean by that a real Teacher of Light), who has an opinion about another individual, is intruding upon that individual's freedom; and it simply should not be done!* One should always guard the thought tenaciously against rebellion of thought when the teaching is presented or good intended; for no one outside of the Arisen Ones is able to judge the intent back of the speech or action.

*The two Wings of the Soul:* It is said or conceded by those of orthodox opinion that Angels have wings. I shall explain to you why. *Determination* and *power* are the two *Wings of the Soul*, not necessarily visible even to the Inner Sight, but they are there just the same. And where you recognize determination as will with its accompanying power, the Soul may rise to any height of Mastery, and in that recognition draw the outer into Itself that there be only *One* — God in Action. The Supremacy of the Mighty Inner Master "Presence" must be acknowledged by the Students as Real and True, and the Students must acknowledge that they have the ability and power to practice that Mighty "Presence" in every act of Life. The more the Students practice the Presence of God within themselves, the easier it becomes and the more they want to practice it. However as I have mentioned many times before, the outer, in the beginning of the advancement, will find every excuse to try to get the attention on outer things or on the body, which in its ignorance it claims as its own.

The only sure release from bodily conditions is to take the mind off the body and keep it off. If there seems to be something that needs correction in the body, put your mind on God and hold it there until the condition that seems to need a remedial agent suddenly disappears. This is why there is now and then a Student who conceives the idea that there is nothing to heal—because anyone who will practice this the instant there seems an appearance in the body of anything discordant, and who will put the mind on God, knows that "Presence" is the most powerful remedial agent in the Universe.

Many, by the use of this Application, will find instant release from any bodily condition that seems inclined to hold the attention. This is, in reality, consciously taking the problem into the Great Silence where there is nothing to heal because all is Perfection. This is just as true of business conditions as for healing the body. In fact, anything that seems to express imperfection can be handled the same way. No permanent release from bodily disturbance can be had, so long as the mind or attention is allowed to be drawn to the condition from which one wishes to be released. With many natures the same thing is true of denials, because the more they deny a thing, the more they bind it to them; for in the denial they are letting their attention rest on the very thing from which they wish release.

To truly practice the Presence of God, we must know that there is only One Intelligence which can act, One Power to use, and One Love with which to accomplish. You know by this that you have within, the Victorious, Conquering Activity every moment. Thus, whenever there is anything to be handled — it matters not what — the moment it seems to have an appearance, using your Wings of Determination and Power, say: *"God, solve this problem and do it at once! I give You all the power where it belongs! I recognize You as the only Activity! Therefore, this appearance has no reality and dissolves instantly before Thy Mighty Presence!"*

If the Students will continually use this, they will soon find that they have no problems. As conditions permit, you will find that this which has been given is but a small part of what may be given for use — as you become more and more aware that you are gaining, not only in what to do, but how to do it. It is the same as with a teacher in the outer schools who gives the child a problem. He also shows the method by which to solve the problem, or he would be a very inefficient teacher indeed.

The Student will always find that where there is sufficient sincerity and earnestness, and a constant calling for Light and Understanding, the Way will always appear for the Knowledge to be given which will lead him or her to Freedom. The True Activity, when we have come to this present state of understanding, is to give no quarter whatsoever to outer appearances.

The Student at this point should constantly analyze the outer — not in a critical way, but that he or she may be conscious of what there is that needs changing. The sincere Student should with all tenacity break up every old personal habit no matter what it is — for that is the thing that binds.

A great many Students do not give this the slightest consideration. The old personal habit is the serpent in the garden, so to speak. This is what I mean by analyzing: to know what there is to break up, which before we have been considering as a necessary habit. There are so many little things in a person's Life which are limitations that can be broken up. We must break up old habits as ice in the springtime, for they form incrustations that prevent proper growth.

When old habits are set, a rebellion in the outer takes place when a change comes; and this always disturbs the feelings. This is one of the greatest unrecognized barnacles of the Soul. There is not one person out of a thousand who has the slightest idea of the number of these old personal habits until he turns about and looks at them; then he can see how these incrustations bind him.

The serpent so-called, which is but rebellion and resentment, will find nothing to feed upon when these habits are broken up. Therefore it will hunt for more fertile fields, or in other words, completely disappear from your garden. If old personal habits are broken up, there is no resistance to the Truth. The right attitude is to joyously accept the Truth, no matter how much it mangles up the outer. This is why we must stand guard every moment at the gate of our outer world.

*The True Activity of Love:* When an individual feels that he or she cannot give forth Divine Love, it is because that one does not understand the True Activity of Love. Where two individuals are concerned—one seeming to be in disgrace while the other so to speak stands guard—a person does not direct the attention to, or attempt to love the discordant thing; but he is to love the Glorious Being imprisoned within the individual, because of Its Perfection and because the discord of the outer self has bound It. The Christ Attitude would be to send Great Love to that imprisoned Presence, which is God—the Light within the individual. This, anyone can do with Great Devotion.

Knowing this, make the Conscious Demand with determination and power, that God break down and dissolve the barrier and set this Radiant Presence free to again assume Its Dominion and create Perfection in Its outer world. The individual standing guard in such a case, has the Divine Right to make this Conscious Demand; and if it is kept up, the way will be opened and the problem solved in the right way. This will give a peace and relief to the one standing guard who really grasps this idea, that will be almost unbelievable. The mistake so many people make is in attempting to solve a condition with the outer mind.

*Enthroning your own Divinity:* The most important and the greatest thing that everyone needs to do, and especially Students who are sincere, is to consciously enthrone their own Divinity in Its Temple, giving all power, all devotion, praise, and recognition to It, that the outer attention may be firmly anchored once and for all time where it belongs. Thus the outer, which has been the usurper, will be drawn into the Great River of Light, until the very existence of the outer is forgotten.

As the autumn approaches, take the conscious stand: *"God, the 'Mighty I AM Presence'! See that every part of my body is governed harmoniously and that I am not affected by atmospheric conditions! God is the Center of my being and governs my body in Perfect Harmony at all times! I do not accept suggestions from those about me, either from the spoken word or from appearances! I move Free! forever Free! in my Mighty 'God Presence'!"*

*Very important:* The conscious recognition of the Electronic Activity within your own body as the Electrons bursting, is a real Activity taking place. The picturing of the Inner Reality becomes Reality in the outer self. The use of the Blue Flame stimulates the Electronic Action within the physical body and ignites the Gold, Pink, and Violet Flame in Its Force Field. This sets these Activities into Action, as the Force from the Electron radiates out. The true nature and color of the Electron is in reality an intense Sapphire Blue; to some it might seem Violet.

It is important to understand at this time, that any Ray having Its own original state of color may be made to contain the Activity of another Ray, by the conscious effort of qualifying It thus. For instance, the Rose-Pink Ray of Love may be touched by the Violet of Power; or the same Ray may be edged on one side with Gold and the other with Violet, which makes the Trinity of Love, Wisdom, and Power.

As you advance in understanding, you will be able to consciously form different combinations as the occasion may require. For instance, as the Ascended Masters operate — and anyone else may if they so choose, the White Ray may be used as the foundation upon which to operate, It being qualified with the other colors and elements as may be required. This places within the hands of the sincere Student almost Limitless Activity and Power.

The Student who constantly asks for Divine Love to enfold and Wisdom to direct the Power he or she uses, will enable this Activity to become so anchored, that after a while the very use of the Rays will naturally call forth Love and Wisdom in Their Action.

As We said in the beginning, when the old personal habits are broken up, you will find them replaced by these Marvelous Divine Habits that will indeed be a True Blessing. One must become aware that in the Mighty Activity of God is all Mentality; and when we mentally connect with an idea, which always has its form, we are in direct communion with the presence of that form.

All Students who come to a certain point of understanding, will come to know that America is to be the Great Jewel of God's Light — I say this advisedly — beyond any part of the Earth!

*Mrs. Ballard:* "Will the pictures of the Arisen Masters be precipitated sometime?"

*Saint Germain:* The time is rapidly approaching when many such things will be done; and the purpose of it is to have anchored in the mind of humanity, the Reality of those Mighty Beings. It is important that humanity realize that there is a Great Host of Advanced Beings beyond this present state—

proving that Life is Eternal, and that from the visible to the invisible is but a slight step anyone might take without passing through the change called death.

*BENEDICTION:* Mighty Presence, Beloved Cherubim! We give praise and thanks for the Wondrous Radiation, for the Blessings that are showered forth today. We give praise and thanks for the Mighty Radiation that has gone forth in official places, preparing the way for God's Messengers to be enthroned for the Dispensation of God's Great Love, Wisdom, and Justice. We give praise and thanks that all mankind have become an Anchorage for the Mighty Presence of God, quickened into the Activity of a Conscious Desire for the Presence of God. We demand that it be quickened with great rapidity to bring forth the full fruition of that which is to be.

# DISCOURSE XIII

*August 15, 1932*

SAINT GERMAIN

*INVOCATION:* Thou Mighty Infinite Presence of Light! We give praise and thanks for Thy Intense Radiation, for the Joy of Thy Great Radiation, for the Peace of Thy Great Love, for the Grace of Thy Eternal Youth made manifest in these forms! Help each one in this, Thy Chosen Center, to feel—to be—Thy Joyous Presence, to know there is naught manifest but the Perfect Activity of God. And give us the Wisdom and Strength to at all times maintain Thy Perfect Harmony, that we may receive the Being and Majesty of Thy Omnipresence.

I bring you Love and Greetings from the Host of Light, who wrap around you Their Mantle of Love that raises the outer into Full Perfection.

## THE DISCOURSE
The beauty of an understanding Heart is without limit; for the endeavor to gain this simple understanding of these Higher Laws so that one may put

them into daily practice, enables the Mighty Master "Presence" to shed Its Fragrance over the lives of those who acknowledge the "Presence," and by this to give every assistance to steady them in the successful application of the understanding they possess from time to time.

In order for the Students or individuals to have the comprehension of the Mighty Force they are using every waking moment, they must try to see wherein and how they are utilizing this stupendous Force. As is often called to the attention of the Students from one source or another, they are constantly sending forth tremendous energy. This, if understood and consciously directed to a given purpose, could not and would not fail in quick accomplishment.

This is rather a savage thing to say, but it is true and must be said: most of the force sent forth by individuals is through anger or resentment, in some of their subtle forms. Why? Because it generates an intense feeling. Anyone who does not understand this or—understanding—does not control it, but delays the hour of achievement. It has been thought by even advanced individuals that it was not possible to generate consciously and at will an intense feeling, according to the desire. I tell you surely and truly that anyone can, if they will, generate the same intensity of feeling for the adherence to the Light that they can generate in a fit of anger, temper, or despondency.

These are the two opposites. To allow oneself to drop into a fit of discouragement or despondency is but letting oneself be used. Instead, one should rise up and utilize his opportunity. He should generate intense love, the opposite pole to his despondency or anger; and through this he would master his problem. However, this is seldom found. But the one who will do it, is always master of every condition.

When the Student who has had many examples before him of the Mighty Activity of the Great Law — God within him — allows depression to engulf him momentarily, he is but expressing a form of self-pity, which should be shunned by the sincere Student as he would shun a poisonous viper.

Students of any understanding to speak of, must know that everything depends upon themselves, and that to form a habit of looking to someone else to sustain them but delays their own Mighty Victorious Accomplishment. Victory over oneself when this constantly generated energy is utilized in this haphazard, thoughtless manner, takes twice as much energy as is otherwise required to sustain them in Perfection, in Health, in Prosperity and Happiness. The Students who want to succeed must face this fact and conquer it in themselves.

Now here is the greatly encouraging thing about this sort of reprimand — which the above might be thought to be, but is not: When the desire of the individual is sent forth or held on constructive accomplishment, he has the Power of the Universe at his back and at his Command, that will sustain him unfailingly in every instance when his determination is held unwaveringly.

Again, let Me remind you that self-pity is the strongest disintegrating force of any one attribute of negative consciousness. When a Student, because things have not been accomplished for him, suddenly takes the attitude, "Why isn't this accomplished now?" — I want to say that this point is not of any consideration if he really wants his manifestation. His part is to stand with firm, unflinching determination to the only Power that ever acts, which is God in himself; and without thought or question of why a thing isn't accomplished, take this stand: *"By the Power of Almighty God in me, I know that whenever I stand with determined desire to accomplish something constructive, it cannot fail."*

The thing that very often causes seeming failure is the very subtle point of wondering why it isn't accomplished yet or doesn't seem to be. Instead of wondering what energy should be sent forth, know that when the Decree has gone forth for any constructive desire, it is God acting. Then of course you must know and feel that it is impossible for It to fail. This is self-evident. Thus, in a simple manner is the consciousness utilizing this Mighty Energy as It should be used.

The following is the reason why Students delay the very thing that they wish to succeed in. As an illustration: if the Student has worked earnestly, knowing the Truth and consciously directing the Power in the right manner, and then if he suddenly allows discouragement or despondency to sweep over him for one hour, he may—according to the intensity of the feeling—dissolve all he has accomplished through days of earnest work. This is a reminder to the Student to stand his ground and never yield or give power to anything but that Mighty Presence of God, which accomplishes all things through His Mighty Presence and Power of Divine Love.

*Read this reminder:* If Students are strong enough to face this Truth—to read this reminder whenever they find themselves slipping—it will be a Limitless Source of Strength and Encouragement to them; for through these Words, to everyone who reads them, will flow a Mighty Sustaining Power.

There is no one thing of greater importance—and yet so simple that a child can comprehend it—than for a Student to watch and see in what manner he is constantly sending forth this Great Energy. The simple, natural manner in which one is constantly giving off, as it were, this force, is quite sufficient for the accomplishment of ordinary things. Then you can readily see what enormous added power and energy is given off by the Conscious Use of the determination and will.

Individuals will often say, "How do I know whether I am using the Inner or outer will?" — when it is so easy to determine, knowing that any constructive desire is the using of the Inner or Divine Will. If Students will accept and utilize these simple yet Mighty Truths, they will find no difficulty in handling themselves or conditions.

While the generation of anger comes of a sudden impulse, the Conscious Use of joyous determination is at least twenty times more effective; and this, one can generate consciously and at will. How? By stilling oneself and joyously entering into the consciousness of how Limitless God's Power is. It is impossible for God to fail in anything, and Its Activity is more or less Instantaneous, in accordance with how much power we withdraw from outer things to which we have given power.

This will show you how one can always have the Power of Accomplishment as the Mighty Magic Wand in one's hands to use for anything whatsoever, from the simplest to the greatest. The only reason for the seeming lack or delay of accomplishment is that one is either consciously or unconsciously dividing this Mighty Power, for it surely does follow and act according to the direction given it.

Meditating upon this and knowing it, will enable the Students to give fuller and fuller power to that Mighty Energy which they may consciously direct at any time. It is when we need the assistance most that we should stand with the greatest determination: for when everything is going joyously, harmoniously, and prosperously, the very forward movement of our being requires very little conscious effort; but when the Students enter onto the Conscious Path, then they have taken the reins and are supposed to consciously direct this Power—and especially when they have dedicated themselves to the Divine Service of the Light.

I say to the beloved Students that this is no idle thing when the Students dedicate themselves to Divine Service. It means that they have thrown down the gauntlet and have challenged battle with the outer self, which *must* be done sometime; and the sooner it is done, the sooner over with. But because the outer form falls down over a secret wire placed there by the outer self, is no reason why one should not get up and go serenely on.

The nature of the individual is such that until he understands these points of vital importance, he does not stop to realize that when everything is going well is the time to build up his momentum and gird himself with the Armor of that Mighty Master "Presence." Then if he finds himself tripped up, this very momentum will cause him to bound like a rubber ball onto his feet, taking quick and powerful command of the situation, commanding this Mighty Presence of God to solve and govern the situation — whatever it may be. Knowing this, you will see and agree with Me how absolutely absurd it is to allow yourself to become negative in the least.

*The positive and negative forces:* Now right here, it is a good thing to understand that the negative and positive forces exist everywhere in Creation; and the negative is in nowise to be condemned, for it is the means by which the Children of Light are caused to become more and more aware of their own Conquering Positive Force. To give way to the negative force is to become more and more enmeshed in it, but to instantly recognize the presence of any negative thought or feeling is but to cause one to turn to one's positive pole and rest there serenely.

*The manifestation:* As We have said before, *the manifestation will come if you want God enough!* It cannot help it! It will fall over itself to get to you if you want God enough. The Students who want to, can take this now and stand their ground. The people wallow in the negative conditions instead of rising up and saying, *"I stand with God and refuse to be affected by this seeming appearance."* If we permit or allow negative conditions to control us, nobody can help us, not even God Himself.

*Beloved Lanto:* Lanto was from this Earth, but He has arisen to Venus and has become the Star Pupil of Sanat Kumara. He is the Ascended Master in charge of the Retreat of the Royal Teton, but was not the Guest Master from Venus. He was the one that introduced the Master from Venus who was the Guest and who was given charge of the evening [see "Venus Visits the Royal Teton," *Unveiled Mysteries*].

*Cherubim:* There are certain Cherubim who have been human, but only a few. There are some from a Sphere of Activity who are prepared with a well-rounded knowledge. Each Element has those of Its own who are sent forth to teach the rest of those in that Element.

*Venus:* Venus came to assist the Earth with Its own Wisdom. Through all Creation, the step higher is always reaching back to the step lower to give assistance.

*The Ascended Masters:* The Ascended Masters teach the inhabitants of the Elements the Laws of

God and Immortality, and thus They prepare those of each Element to teach the rest in that Element.

*Retreats in the mountains:* The early Power used by the Ascended Masters in preparing Retreats in the mountains, had to be secret and not discoverable by anyone in the outer world. The Great Watcher saw the necessity of the Great Light having Indestructible Protection. This is why there were Retreats in all parts of the World in caves and mountains. They used the Flame to break down the great masses of rock, and the elementals were created for the purpose of disposing of the debris. Later all was disintegrated by a Flame.

*The Raising of the body before the Advent of the Master Jesus:* Up until the Advent of Beloved Jesus, all raising of the body was an absolutely secret process. Not even the Students in association knew what was to be done — only the one raising or being assisted in the Raising.

*Age of the Earth:* Human Life has been on this Earth since it was created. Geologists only have an approximate idea of the age of the Earth, unless they have been highly inspired.

*Former civilizations:* All evidence of some former, great civilizations has disappeared except certain records. There came a time when indestructible receptacles had to be prepared by Precipitation for the preservation of certain records of former civilizations.

There will yet be a Chamber of Records that will be unsealed, when the New Age has been entered into sufficiently and the Christ Power has gained sufficient Dominion. This Chamber will reveal another period of civilization's progress, far greater than the one known at present.

In the Inner Cosmic Activity, you will see the Creative Process of God. You are the Eternal Wisdom of the Eternal Creative Process acting, as far as you have gone. That is why knowing a thing in this manner means that you have entered into the Creative Process, and this Knowledge is different from any other kind of knowledge.

*Ascent of the Soul:* There were points of rest for the descent and Ascent of the Soul in its intense outer activity.

*The Akashic Records machine:* The machine to read the Akashic Records will not come forth until humanity is sufficiently evolved to hold to the Christ Presence with no danger of slipping back. If this instrument were to come forth now, it would upset every theory the scientific world has.

The only thing anyone has to do is to anchor into God and stay there, and human beings will continue to suffer until this is done. The process of gaining Self-consciousness would be impossible without reembodiment. The outer body could not stand the speed of evolving Self-conscious knowledge in one body.

*Notes and Affirmations:*

" 'Mighty I AM Presence,' give me Thy Foresight and guard all future activity, that everything concerning it may be maintained harmoniously."

"In the Fullness of the 'Presence' is the thing that I desire."

At least once a day, demand that your world be flooded with the Mightiest Activity of Divine Love.

"God, the 'Mighty I AM Presence,' surround and protect me from every outer vibration."

" 'I AM' always Christ Victorious!"

When one starts to argue with you for a negative thing, take a definite stand and make them realize that they are arguing for the very thing they do not want.

God is alive within you. Do not allow Him to be silenced by the doubts and fears and uncertainties of the human self! Obedience is the most important of all things.

Beloved Nada; Mary, the Mother of Jesus; and Meta, the Mother of Cha Ara are definitely concerned with the Motherhood of humanity.

*BENEDICTION:* Mighty "Presence"! We give praise and thanks for Thy Radiation ever active in these lives and this home. Make it such a Radiant Center that all are blest who come into it.

# DISCOURSE XIV

*August 18, 1932*

SAINT GERMAIN

*INVOCATION:* Thou Mighty Impelling Force and Intelligence governing Thy Wonderful Creation, animate and inanimate, We give praise and thanks for that Great Privilege of being in Thy Great Individualization. We give praise and thanks that We have within Our Consciousness Thy Presence centered there All-powerfully — All-intelligently governing all substance so that We may command and be obeyed.

We give praise that We are One with Thee, Almighty Father, and that it is not a dream that We are Children of the Mighty God. We do have Thy Mighty Power to use for Almighty Good. May Thy Wisdom guide, Thy Light enfold, and Thy Intelligence direct Us unerringly that We may enter quickly into Thy Eternal Perfection.

I bring you Love and Greetings from the Host of Light and the friendly Deva. This Deva was much pleased that this Good Brother was able to see the

Overshadowing Radiation. There is One at present overshadowing Chicago, maintaining Its Radiation here.

## THE DISCOURSE

It seems to Me that it would be well to have a clearer understanding of the activity of Free Will. Children as a rule choose their parents, those to whom they shall be born in this earthly Life. Those who are to do Special Work are sometimes assisted by the Great Ones in making their choice. No one can be blamed for conditions, except the individual himself. No child can blame the parent for anything. No individual can blame anyone but himself for what seems to be lacking in this matter.

Energy is always present in great abundance; but if not rightly used, things cannot be accomplished. Any affliction within the individual is his or her own creation. This must be recognized by Students so there will be no drifting away from their own responsibility.

Every individual is a God in embryo and can call forth Limitless Power to use for his advancement at any and all times. The cause of one's seeming slowness of advancement, many times, is because the Student or individual is consciously or unconsciously looking for the manifestation rather than the joy of entering into the Great Heart of God's Great Silence. If once the Students truly understand this, it opens a new gateway to their growth and causes them to look entirely within themselves for everything. The inclination of the human or outer activity to continually be looking for something *outside* upon which to blame their own shortcomings, is the great stumbling block to the rapid progress of many.

I am clearly aware of the great controversy which existed at one time over the idea of Free Will, but that does not alter the Truth in any way. I tell you, everyone has Free Will and is commanded to choose whether they shall serve the Upward or downward course; and no one can say them nay in their own choice. Those who choose the Upward Path have the Mighty Presence, Intelligence, and Power of the Ascended Host and the Great Devas to assist them in every manner that is permissible.

Again, it is well to remind the earnest Student to keep looking to and asking the Mighty "Presence" to show him clearly the Way and to answer his questions—because if the Student will sincerely ask that Mighty Inner "Presence" to do it, those questions will be answered; and after a few experiences, he will find the answers coming quickly and surely. Such effort will give the added impetus and stimulus to make this an easy and continuous activity.

The sincere Student should call on the Law of Forgiveness every day, and give praise and thanks for having come to the point of consciously knowing the Mighty God within.

*The Deva:* The Mighty Deva who has so wondrously chosen to come and minister, making this a most unusual Center of Radiation, is a Deva from the Temple of Green. The Deva ministers for the purpose of stimulating the Inner or Divine Activity into a certain definite action — not only for the Students who come within Its Radiance, but to the city of Chicago and to North America.

*The mountain in Alaska:* It is not generally known, in fact not known in the outer world at all, that at the time the top of the mountain was blown off in Alaska, there were certain chemicals and forces liberated from the Earth that temporarily dulled the activity of a large portion of mankind; and I wish to state that it was not an ordinary volcanic eruption.

*The Great Depression [1929]:* The time has arrived when the depression is being and will be completely removed. The so-called depression that reached its lowest ebb some time ago is the result of this activity in Alaska. But, as is always the case, the Great Wisdom of the Ascended Host and Their Messengers, the Ascended Masters, always finds means of transmuting a thing that might be harmful into ultimate good. This is applicable to an individual as well as to a nation. The momentum of the so-called depression, I assure you, is completely broken; and as the ice breaks up in the springtime thaw, so is it being scattered, dissipated, and dissolved into its nothingness. The volcanic explosion in Alaska affected the World War also.

Through the Mighty Radiation and Lifting Process of the Ascended Host, Their Assistance will cause a quickening and clearness of activity in the outer thought of mankind. This will surprise even those to whom it comes. It will be as though they are awakening from a dream.

Let Me again urge each one that when a disturbing thought comes, you put it out of your mind instantly and do not accept it or allow it to get whirling into a momentum. Instead say: *"Get out! There is only God and His Perfect Activity in My Life, home, and affairs."* Keep up your work in knowing: *"There are no personalities here! There is only God in Action everywhere present."* This is a positive form, recognition, and acceptance of the Mighty "God Presence," even though you are not having the attention on the thought of Protection.

*Love:* Love, being the Hub of the Universe, is naturally the cohesive element and is the Power that projects into form. If people do not love enough — or not at all — they are shunned by everything, for they repel; those who love, attract. The very energy Students use to criticize or condemn, if turned to the Mighty "Presence," would not only give them relief, but would set into motion Great Light and Understanding. We are all using enormous energy all the time, and the thoughtless use of it is enough to move a mountain. The Power is in these Words and there is no mistake about it, if the Student will accept it.

The Mighty Stream of Life flows ceaselessly on, and it is so easy to enter that Stream and Its Perfect Action in the Recognition and Acceptance of that Mighty Presence of God in us. The minute we deny or doubt, we turn ourselves out of this Stream. All discord is but to call the attention to the fact that the outer, or human self, has turned out of It. The moment one entertains discordant thoughts and feelings, he has turned out of the Stream, and the discord continues to build.

There will come a machine for the directing of certain colors, charged and qualified by the individual operating the machine.

*Dinosaurs:* There was a great mass-thought or desire for drawing this atomic structure into form. By drawing certain foci into these large forms, it was much more quickly accomplished than otherwise would have been. In the beginning these animals were not vicious, and they were entirely subservient to the direction of the individual. They were very friendly, as were all those giant creations originally. In that period, a great activity took place in drawing together large quantities of the atomic structure. There existed great love between them and the human; and thus, the process of raising it was very rapid. There is so much concerning these previous civilizations which is not known today, that the outer world only has a fragmentary idea regarding that entire activity.

*The Great Central Sun:* The Truth is that the Great Central Sun is a Presence, a Form, and a Place within the Center of Creation, radiating in all directions. I assure you It is a very Tangible Place, a Mighty and Tremendous Reality.

*Beloved Surya:* The Ascended Master Surya is really the Lord Maitreya, and from that Great Presence was the planetary action of Surya established. Surya is a Constellation as well as a Great Cosmic Master. All astronomical names and activity come from Individuals, or come from the Intelligent Activity of God within the Individuals. All were named after those Individuals who had much to do with their Manifestation. The name "Maitreya" contains a certain activity.

*Mrs. Ballard:* "Is Its use the release of a certain Force with the Quality of Love—and certain other Attributes, the Power within It?"

*Saint Germain:* All names used for astronomical purposes contain within them certain and very definite Activity.

*Astrology and its use:* All negative interpretation of astrology is only what individuals give it. The original reality and use of astrology was that it drew the attention of certain Great Beings to whom the individual was somewhat naturally attuned, that he might receive the Radiation and uplift of the Great Beings. The idea that individuals are affected by the radiation of a Planet, which is in nowise a personal force, is—from the standpoint of reality—a perfectly absurd thing. For a force to operate, it must have intelligence back of it. Consequently, knowing that God is the All-acting Power in the Universe, then We know that the Quality from any Planetary Intelligence can only be good, unless the mind of the individual requalifies it.

The present astrology is a constant throwing of obstacles into the path of the individual. The idea that one of God's days is any more or less perfect than another for the activity of God's Children, is the most absurd thing imaginable. I am amazed that people's thought is so shallow that they do not think this through and see the absurdity of it.

*Take your questions to your God Self:* If the individual would take his or her stand upon any question in the mind and say, *"God, show me and tell me the Truth about this thing,"* it would start an activity that would bring the full explanation. One must hold fast until the answer comes, for it always will. If one wants to go downtown, he continues until he arrives there. It is the same activity that is needed with mental work. When one starts a thing, he should continue on the way until he attains it.

It seems so strange that individuals will not hold fast to the idea and use of the God Quality in everything about them, instead of trying to requalify it themselves. However, if the Student of understanding sees a wrong condition, then by knowing that *"there is only God in Action"*--it might be considered qualifying, but it is really loosing the God Power into action within it. This is really not requalifying, but instead is using the God Quality already there. Regardless of what is taking place, all energy is God's Energy. If people accepted the natural quality within, they would find it is really God. If they would know but this, it would be recognizing the True Quality, and so only God could come back to them.

*The animal element:* The substance that came

into form was at one time far denser than now. The animal element that came through the lower activity, or the conscious lowering to creating for pleasure, caused the creation of the animal form in the atomic structure of the outer world. In other words, the bodies of animals are the objectification of the thoughts and feelings held in the outer consciousness of human beings when they created simply for the gratification of appetite and pleasure sensation.

*An Eternal Truth:* The human Soul never evolves through the animal. The outer atomic structure is but the raised or prepared condition for it, to be used in the forming of human bodies. This is nearing the last step from the atomic into the Electronic Structure.

The human Soul came directly from God. Therefore it could not have evolved out of the group soul of the animal. The human Soul must go back to God. Understanding the absolute certainty of the Law of Free Will, the "Law of the Expression of the Fullness of God," it must go through every phase of experience, attaining again that Perfection through the conscious understanding of all phases of Life's Activity.

At the time Free Will was given to the Individualization—certainly not unknowingly of what would come—knowing there were two opposites throughout all lower manifestation, the Soul went forth to conquer all negative conditions and again return to that Perfect State, crowned with the Victory of Self-conscious Knowledge. This is why one cannot learn from another's experience. Each must go through all experience and conquer himself or herself. That is the reason for the long process of re-embodiment, for the Soul has to have periods of rest from this intense activity.

This is why no Arisen Master ever has such a thing as a condemnatory thought—for They have gone through all experience in order to come to the Arisen State. This, however, does not mean in every detail. The power through Self-conscious Knowledge, gained through the Life of experience, gives one infinitely greater capacity, greater understanding, greater power than one who has never come into it at all. This is why one who has come down through the human experience and by self-effort has raised himself to become an Ascended Being, is Master over even the Angel Devas. There are some Angel Devas who have been through the human experience.

*Coming Life of the Angels:* There will come a time in a very much higher phase of the experience Life, when the Angels who have never humanly embodied will come forth and, through certain Memory

Records of this present Life experience, will be taught these things on a higher scale and with a speed that is hardly conceivable in the present day.

*Affirmations:*

" *'I AM' the 'Presence' that disconnects my being and world from the magnetic pull of Earth and all human creation.* "

" *'I AM' the 'Presence' that frees me from any condition.* "

*BENEDICTION:* Mighty Cherubim — Mighty Presence of the Messengers of God! We give praise and thanks for the Outpouring this day and that Thou hast reached over all of North America, unclothing Thy Power there, giving Clearness and Free Dominion of thought to mankind. We give praise and thanks that this Mighty Activity has been accomplished. See that this Mighty Work goes on until the Emancipation of mankind is completed.

# DISCOURSE XV

*August 22, 1932*

SAINT GERMAIN

*INVOCATION:* Thou Wondrous, Mighty Creator of all that is—animated by Thy Mighty Energy ever flowing through Thy Heart! We give praise and thanks for the Outpouring of Thy Mighty Love, Wisdom, and Power, Thy Mighty Supply ever present. All-active is Thy Mighty Substance, waiting to be acted upon by the consciousness of the Children of Earth. We give praise and thanks for Thy Radiant Presence, ever quickening into activity Thy Particles of Thyself—the Electron—causing It to shed Its Radiance more and more brilliantly everywhere for Thy Activity through Nature in the minerals and rocks.

We give praise and thanks for the "Gem of America" lying in the Heart of Thy Presence, awaiting the hour to fulfill Thy Majestic Plan, pouring out to the Children of Earth Thy Mighty Grace and Activity that will be the Central Gem in Thy Crown, radiating Goodwill to man. We praise Thee, Thou

King of Kings, that all be Thy Mighty Messengers, parts of Thyself, and for the part of Thyself that causes Us to know the Factor in all Life. Strengthen Thy Children that they may hold steadfast in Thy Mighty Radiance, in Peace and Blessing to mankind and all the Earth.

I bring you Greetings and Blessings from the Cherubim, the Deva, and the Ascended Host!

### THE DISCOURSE

I bring you triple Greetings and Blessings from the Cherubim and the Deva and the Ascended Host, who give Their Praise and Encouragement to you for the unasked aid in holding the Mighty Focus wherein the Power of the Music was sent forth to all the Earth — to heal, to bless, to bring Peace, and to prosper. It is one thing to give praise and assistance when asked, and a far greater thing to sense it and give without being asked. Give forth praise and recognition of this Blessing constantly; and from this day forth, you will find a great change taking place in all your affairs.

The Music Festival of Chicagoland was the greatest opportunity of its kind on Earth for radiating the Light from the Ascended Host to a great number of humanity. Up to this time, the opportunity of radiating through the Passion Play of Oberammergau was the greatest, outside of the Retreats. Many people unknowingly have been awakened while absorbing the "Presence" during the Passion Play.

The commercial world is sometimes foolish enough to think that a Divine Radiation may be transferred from one continent to another to gratify its ambitious vanity. When something is established for a special Purpose, if the time arrives when it can no longer be utilized, the Power and Force are withdrawn.

*The Music Festival's Inner Activity:* I feel certain that this important activity of *The Chicago Tribune* will open the way for Mighty Inner Power to flow into its activity. Whether this is done from the outer or Inner activity, is not important; it is worthy of great Inner Commendation. As the immense billows of created color from the Music rose in great castle-like shapes and stood there in their vibrant color of Active Life, the Mighty Cherubim, Deva, and Ascended Host created a Mighty Pillar of Light, white in color—raising It to the Height of the Cherubim, from which Its Rays, colored by the consciousness of the requirement, were sent forth to all parts of the Earth—especially encompassing America, touching the Hearts and consciousness of many individuals throughout the Land, who, it is seen from the higher standpoint, will become Messengers of the Light.

*The Activity sent forth by the Deva:* The Activity sent forth by the Deva was from the Jade Temple of Light, causing the quickening of the Inner Activity of individuals everywhere that were in anywise prepared to receive It.

*The Activity of the Cherubim:* The Activity of the Cherubim was from the Golden Temple of Light, raising the attunement of the mentality of individuals everywhere who could be raised.

*The Activity of the Ascended Host:* Seven of the Ascended Host, acting from the Violet Temple of Light, sent forth Mighty Rays, commanding Obedience to the Inner Activity of Divine Forces acting everywhere on the physical plane. Here may I say that all acceptance of the Mighty Truth and Its Activity, by the Student or individual, must always be voluntary. The more intense the joy reaching out for Light and Understanding, the more is It hastened into activity in the individual's Life and world. The more one accepts the Inner Truth as a Reality, the more that one can be used as a Mighty Messenger of the Light.

So much is to be given of this Mighty Inner Truth that will strain the credulity of even the most sincere Student, that nothing but the Inner Prompting of the individual's own God within will make it possible for him to accept. Nothing will be given except verifiable Truth; yet there will be many who, not yet having reached quite the point of assimilation, may think some things quite farfetched. But that will be unfortunate for them. No longer, in the Mighty Radiation of this Inner "Presence," is the growth of the individual to be considered; but the Radiance will pour forth, clothing humanity in Its close Embrace.

Those who have an awakened understanding to grasp the import of this Mighty Activity in their individual lives and in the world at large, will find a speed of activity in their own consciousness that will at times quite amaze them. Thus, it behooves every sincere Student to reach for the Light with all the strength and sincerity at his or her command, so that they may share and utilize this Great Glory of God showered upon Earth, clothing the Children of God with such Light as the Earth has not known before. We have determined that this thought, feeling, and expression of depression shall fade away from the minds of mankind and be replaced by courage, strength, and confidence.

*The Way to Freedom:* Again let Me say with great emphasis, that the perfect and quickest way to Freedom is the feeling of constantly moving in the Radiance and Intelligence of God. Consciously fill yourself, your mind and body, so full of God that there isn't room for anything else. Guard yourself and do not give quarter to any kind of feeling that is less than All of God.

*Those who may walk and talk with God:* At various periods during the past centuries, especially the earlier centuries, it was an acknowledged fact that a few of humanity walked and talked with God. I assure you for your encouragement, that there are ten times the number of people today walking and talking with God, who, if they could cast off the outer effect of human fear and suggestion, might easily equal those of the past who walked and talked with God. Those of former times were absolutely fearless, even concerning their own lives and liberty; consequently, they opened wide the Door for that Mighty Flow of God's Activity through them.

The people of today have too much reticence in sharing their experience of the many wondrous things they have received; because of human opinions, in most instances they have held these locked within their own Hearts, lest they should be ridiculed. When one is consciously with God, moving in His Mighty Presence, why should that one fear what any man might say? It is he who bears false witness that should fear — not the Messenger of Truth; for at this time, instead of the Messenger of Truth being burned at the stake, the one who bears false witness or attempts to interfere is the most liable to be scorched by the Inner Fire, the Flame of God. In these days, the Messengers of Light always draw to themselves their own—in other words, those who are ready to receive the River of Light that is poured forth through the Messengers.

No one will be urged or carried, but each must come from his or her own joyous desire, knowing that God in each one is his own Self-sustaining Power. It is now important to utilize every channel to pour forth the Radiation of Light, to hasten the adjustment of things and conditions. When the wedge has once been driven and can be followed up by the conscious cooperation of a few of the Children of Light, then the barrier of human thought is torn asunder and cast aside, and the River of Light pours forth on Its way. In this case, the River of Light is not destructive, while the river of water may be.

However, you will notice in all the great avenues of progress that at the times when there seemed to have been destructive forces at work, it was but the coarser element giving way and being replaced by the Activity of Higher Attunement. I trust that each of you will feel the Great Joy that I feel in these accomplishments, not only in your own activity but in that which has gone forth to bless mankind.

*For keeping awake:* If you find yourself feeling drowsy when you wish to work, command the cause to be consumed, that you may stand free to do that which you wish to do.

*For going to sleep:* Command through your Mighty Inner "Presence" that when you wish to sleep you are held in that "Presence" — Invincible — and that the body sleeps as an infant. Know always that you are God commanded, so you guard yourself that you do not give power unknowingly to any outer thing. No matter what is attempted by the outer, it has no power unless it be of God.

*Command as Christ:* When you command from the Christ Standpoint, only Christ-like results can follow. Of that you can be absolutely certain, because when you command as the Christ, you immediately cause the *Inner* Activity to take place. It shuts off the outer, using it only as a vehicle of conveyance. As you continue consciously to fill your thought, mind, and body full to overflowing with God, you will find that you are utilizing an Invincible Armor that will build into a Permanent Guard of your thought and intellect.

Until one has had the experience of seeing One appear from the Invisible, there is always a startled feeling the first time it occurs.

The Radiation from the blue costumes at the Music Festival was very powerful because the Blue Ray was used intensively. The Blue Ray is always used to disintegrate the coarser or lower human element.

Beloved Lanto is always in charge of the Retreat at the Royal Teton. You will find during the next seven years, specific Activity among the Ascended Masters. Those having Special Qualities will be called upon for specific Activity, because of Their own Natural Quality.

I shall have to leave you, as I have a long way to go—to the Andes. It is quite nice, after all, to go about without having to pay carfare. The transfer may require two, three, four, or seven minutes to make the change of distance. At first one does not have the sense of going through space; but later on We do see, the same as you do.

*BENEDICTION:* We give praise and thanks for the Mighty Radiant "Presence" that ever ministers to the Messengers of Light, which is ever shedding Courage to bless and sustain them in their Pilgrimage on the Pathway of Light. We give praise and thanks to the Great Centers of Light that have been pleased by the Radiation from this Center, ever shedding Thy Radiance through this Center to mankind, that all may be lifted up to Thee.

Our Beloved Ascended Master Saint Germain

May De Camara 1953

# DISCOURSE XVI

*August 25, 1932*

SAINT GERMAIN

*INVOCATION:* Thou Mighty Creative Principle of Life! As a part of Thee, We give praise and thanks for the recognition of the opportunity of proving Our Inheritance—that We have become conscious We are a part of Thee, and Thy Love, Wisdom, and Power are ever flowing; that this Step through the veil of matter is so easy; that We are always confident We can step through the veil of matter at will, thereby releasing Thy Power into instant Activity; and that Thy Wisdom directs, Thy Love enfolds, and Thy Light protects Thy Children. Let Thy Radiance enfold the mind of every one of Thy Children and cause them to consciously rise into Oneness with Thee.

Greetings and Love from the Host whose Radiation ministers through this Center.

## THE DISCOURSE

*Through the veil:* Within the consciousness of everyone is the Secret Key by which each may go through the veil and become active in his or her own Mighty Inner "Presence," which knows no limitation. Meditate upon this often. We have but to turn this Key and feel and hear the bolt turned back, admitting us to that Chamber of Eternal Silence where the Almighty Creative Power of God is in Action. God has so graciously provided this Key within the consciousness of everyone. How do you turn this key? A simple way is to know that *where your consciousness is, there you are.*

Strange to say, few seem able to accept this Great Truth. I mean by that, to go consciously through and partake of that Great "Presence," which would beautify the body, giving it Eternal Youth; would loose the Wisdom of the Eternal Memory, consciously taking Command; and would make the individual the master of all conditions which God intended His Creation to be master of, and to do all He intended His Creation to do. In the early part of one's Awakening, it requires tenacity to hold fast to the simple things that later seem so powerful. There is no such thing in Our vocabulary as the recognition of the word "can't," when one has learned to follow the Middle Way.

There is, within the consciousness of every individual, that which represents the pendulum of a clock or the Balance of Consciousness. While yet within the hold of human consciousness, the inclination is to swing from one extreme to the other, from great depression to great joy and back again. To consciously take the determined stand that you constantly act within this Perfect Balance of Love, Wisdom, and Power, will enable anyone to come quickly into the poise of the Middle Way and have no fear of swinging to either extreme.

In the control of the waterpower of your physical world, you have gates by which you control its flow. So, within the consciousness of each individual is that Gate of Pearl which it is possible to raise at will, letting through the River of Life, causing it to flow when and where you will, or where there is need or demand. This can be quickly acquired when one is able to shut out the questioning of the outer mind. All accomplishment comes through the steadfastness and unwavering consciousness — paying no attention to the outer appearances, nor setting a time for results.

*Memorize this marvelous Affirmation:* It seems incredible that there must be a continual reminder before the outer consciousness to keep it from running off the track and causing the waste and outlet of the accumulated power. Say tenaciously to every intrusion of the outer mind: *"NO! Absolutely NO! I have been affected and led by your ignorance for the*

*last time! I have entered into my Divine Inheritance
and 'Presence.' Henceforth my attention does remain There, and all the outer screaming for attention I no longer hear. I have entered within the
Sacred Circle of my Mighty Master God Self, and
henceforth naught else but that 'Presence' ever finds
recognition from me!"*

*Faith:* Faith is always an important factor in gaining the use of the Light. As an illustration: if you
were going some place where you had not yet been,
you would have seen a map, heard a description, or
in some other way have learned of this outer place to
which you were going, having perfect confidence
that the place was there. Underlying this activity, the
whole thing is faith in some kind of a report brought
to you. Can you not have this same unwavering confidence and faith in the use of these Super Powers of
which you have heard, although you may not have
yet seen Them? If you would exert the same confidence and faith in reaching to and attaining the Perfect Contact with your Mighty God Self that you
have in physically reaching a destination where you
have not yet been, you would find the results a thousand times more wonderful. You would consciously
reach that Inner "Presence" with far greater invincible certainty than you would the culmination of
your outer journey.

The fact is that in almost every walk of Life, we have a certain confidence that we can go to, do, and be certain things in the outer. Why not have the same confidence in reaching the Inner Light, which brings you rewards so much greater than the outer that there is no comparison? In some way, the Students must gain this certain, invincible confidence in their ability to right now step through the veil and enter into the Full Activity of their Mighty Invincible God Self. They need to do but a small analysis of their own activity, to see how they may turn this mighty confidence and faith into the right and greater channel and have perfect, eternal results, which the activity of the outer self can never give.

Try to recognize that in the slightest activity in the outer, it is always the Power or Energy of God acting. Know this! Then stimulate the activity of the consciousness into recognizing that as you consciously direct this God Power into the channel of your highest desires, you can enter into Its Limitless Use. You do this by recognizing that It is All-powerful and that *through your own consciousness* you give It full Power. This will bring the focus of using your God Power under your conscious, demanded direction, so that instead of many outlets, there is but the single outlet upon which It is focused. By this you know it is impossible not to attain the desired results.

Students everywhere, especially long for Perfection of form, of voice, of activity — when the only thing that stands between them and this Perfection is their own lack of unwavering confidence in the Inner God Power, which is the Life flowing through their forms to produce this desired effect right now.

*Marvels:* Do I startle you when I say that one minute a day of actually, joyously feeling this Mighty Perfection of God permeating your mind and being with Its Full Intensity, would in a few months transmute and transform your entire outer appearance? Strange to say, there is only now and then one who will stay close enough to this simple thing to produce these glorious results. The same may be achieved in the use of this great Love, Wisdom, and Power. Do not wait for something to demand it; but continuously, every time you have a few moments during the day, do the following: Just be still and feel this Perfection of God filling every cell of your being, mind, and body; and you will soon see sufficient results to go joyously on until the complete transformation takes place.

Most individuals, after a few times, a few days, and at most a few weeks, find the joyous enthusiasm waning; and the first thing they know, they have dropped the idea entirely — only because the restless outer has in some way gained their attention. I tell you, Beloved Students, there is no use delaying the Day of Attainment. If you need to renew a garment or you have a desire for a certain kind of food, you find no effort in holding fast to the idea until it comes. It is no harder to enter into the full Illumination of the Light, which contains the Essence of all outer form, and have that Perfect Manifestation in your Life — than it is to get the food or clothing. I leave it to you. Is it not a much more worthy effort?

Again let Me give a simple illustration: In your schoolwork in the outer Life, you are requested to commit to memory a page or a few pages of something. It never occurs to you that you cannot do it. You buckle down to it, and before you can scarcely realize it, it is accomplished. With the same determination, you can restore the forgotten memory that will restore to you great Treasures of Wisdom. I am determined to get the simplicity of this Mighty Truth to you in such a manner that the outer is compelled to give way before this Mighty "Presence." It is but a matter of holding fast until you do accomplish it, and of not letting the outer things switch you off.

As We said in the beginning, a definite Work is being done through this Instruction of the "I AM," and It cannot be undone. The Inner Work of releasing the Great Cosmic Light for the Blessing of mankind, goes on regardless of all outer conditions. This Work is not an ordinary thing, and when the Students come under this Observation, there will be the Irresistible Power of Cosmic Light and Love drawing them; and the moment they begin to turn right or left away from It, they will find something confronting them. When they would forget the Inner Glory of their "Mighty I AM Presence" for the outer, they will find they cannot do it. You see, the fact is that they have entered into the Activity of the Great Love, Wisdom, and Conscious Power of the "Mighty I AM Presence" and the Great Host of Ascended Masters, and that Mighty Activity is All-controlling and Eternal. Once the Great Inner Power, which is the "Mighty I AM Presence," starts to act, in reality It never stops. These individuals have said they wanted to serve the Great Light. It has taken them at their word and goes on!

*Mrs. Ballard:* "Might I sometime serve the Great Powers of Nature by helping to design and create flowers with markings and points of Light as part of them?"

*Beloved Saint Germain:* You are touching a memory of what may again be, but also the memory of what has been.

*Mrs. Ballard:* "Was that on this Earth or on Venus?"

*Saint Germain:* Everywhere. You may do whatever you wish, and none may say you nay. In contemplating this, you are touching your own Divine Element. You see, the Children of the Fire and Air have great genius in the creation of flowers, a process which involves the handling of colors.

There is a school just behind the veil of human limitations, where little children are received and taught. In this school, flowers are created and many things are designed for their education and enjoyment. You teach in this school; and while the verbal instruction is going on, the thought is presented in colors in the most beautiful forms. You have been working in this school for some time, and your coming is looked forward to with great delight by the children.

In the Ascended State all decorative ornamentation is created within the substance itself. For instance, in the building of walls: whatever you determine upon manifests as the finished product; for in the Higher Spheres of Activity, the Eternal Electronic Substance responds as readily to your thought as bread dough does to the activity of your hands on the physical plane. This Eternal Electronic Substance may be molded by thought into the most beautiful forms.

*Mrs. Ballard:* "Will you focus the Light and

Power through and around me strong enough for me
to be the Example of the Fulfillment of the Law?"

*Saint Germain:* Much will come forth in the use
of certain ones. In this Advent of the Mighty "Presence," there will come the demonstrative Power to
prove the Power of God, wherever desirable. You
and this Good Brother, Guy W. Ballard, have both
felt this for some time past. A certain amount of
demonstration in the future will be permitted in
order to more clinchingly hold the attention of the
earnest Student on the Great Law of the "Mighty
I AM Presence."

Every one of God's Children, if they have sufficient determination to utilize the Great Law of God
to heal, bless, and prosper all, will find themselves
able to do amazing things. It is all a matter of reaching into that "Presence" and the Light of the
"Mighty I AM" with sufficient intensity.

If you take a dull coal of fire from the grate and
blow continuously upon it, it will come into a white
heat or light. So does the attention on the Light and
the Mighty Presence of God which you are, cause the
Inner Breath of God to breathe out—or forth, as it
were—causing the Electronic structure of your mind
and body to glow with unusual Radiance. You will
find many wonderful and beautiful things occurring
in your midst.

The True, Secret, Inner Feeling and Attitude of the Student is to take the determined stand that *"there is nothing too great for my attainment"*—and hold fast to it. Then you open wide the Door for marvelous things to appear and occur. The Dove represents the Speed of the Inner Activity. It shows that the True Activity is gaining.

*Contemplate and meditate upon this often:* Any Ascended Master can appear and precipitate this, that, or anything. Say often: *"I can and do precipitate whatever I want. The Inner knows the Perfection and has precipitated the outer."* Know that you can restore that Perfection where It belongs. I never waste time or energy on the inconsistency of human beings; if people want to love their chains, let them have them. Never let the thought or feeling of, "I wonder if it were so?" come into your consciousness. Kick it out forever!

I want to convey to you somehow that each one of you has the power to enter into the God Self when and where you will, for the accomplishment of any good purpose. Make your outer mind continually acknowledge this: *" 'I AM' through the veil now."* Cut off this outer thing that keeps saying you are not.

*The Temples of Light:* There is a vast difference between the Green Temple and the Jade Temple. The Ruby Temple has nothing whatsoever to do with the so-called red of your World, but has Its own special Activity. The Violet Temple is the most marvelous, Divine thing possible to conceive. Then there is the Crystal Temple in which at times the most delicate colors of Ruby, Jade, and Violet play. These four Temples form the corners of the Squaring of the Circle.

*Mrs. Ballard:* "Can we go and visit these Temples at will?"

*Saint Germain:* Positively, just the same as the boys went the other night to the concert. Give the Command, " *'I AM' going to consciously visit and bring back the conscious memory of It.* " Just because you do not always bring back the memory of an experience, is no proof that you did not have it or go where the thought was directed. You do go where the thought is directed. That Truth is Eternal.

Get the Truth fixed forever in your consciousness that when you give a Command as Christ, the Command is fulfilled; for God is the Power acting. Get away from all this wishy-washy doubt. It must be done. Doubt is like being tied to a rubber band. It lets you get away just so far and then pulls you back. Visualize yourself cut free from every limitation. Using your Sword of Blue Flame of Divine Love, make the physical motions. Do not allow yourself to get lukewarm about anything. Keep up a Joyous

Enthusiasm for that Magnificent, Eternal "Presence." Remember that in all Activity done for another by the Ascended Host, it is always done through the Inner Radiance of the Student or individual.

*To Mrs. Ballard:* Centuries ago you precipitated paintings of a Perfection that has never been equaled since. Those transferred from the Temple at Mitla and taken to the Royal Teton were your work.

*To Mrs. Ballard regarding the Retreat:* The Retreat in the Andes is the Retreat of the golden-haired Masters from the Great Central, Spiritual Sun. Remember always to know that after you have given out references about the Ascended Masters, it has anchored within the Student a clearer conception about Them. The recognition of the Ascended Masters and Their Work is a tremendous opportunity for Them to pour forth Help to the Student.

*Please get this:* A Student or individual must first go out in consciousness to an Ascended Master or Great Intelligence; then that Intelligence can come back tenfold or more. It is the same with everything else: until you can recognize that a thing is a fact, how can you receive its benefit?

I must leave you now as I have received My second call. I am going to Switzerland.

There will come forth aerial transportation that will put all other transportation on the rubbish pile, so far as commercial purposes are concerned.

*BENEDICTION:* Mighty "Presence" and Thou Glorious, Radiant Being, Cyclopea, We give thanks for Thy Outpouring, and that Thou dost continue to enfold all in Thy Great Love, Wisdom, and Power. Pour out for these Thy Children, Limitless Supply and Blessings of Earth.

# DISCOURSE XVII

*August 29, 1932*

SAINT GERMAIN

*INVOCATION:* Thou "Mighty Majestic I AM Presence"! God in Action—We give praise and thanks for the Fullness of Thy Perfection made manifest everywhere. Out of the fullness of Thy Life is the River of Peace ever flowing to enfold mankind. Make these Thy Children ever abundantly receptive to Thy Presence. Hold their attention fixed upon Thee, for Thou art the only Eternal Happiness.

Let Thy Wisdom ever fill their minds, directing them in the Perfect Way Thou dost wish them to go. Let them *feel* Thy Majesty in their consciousness. Let them be conscious that Thou art holding them within Thy Magic Circle centered within Thy Heart, that Thy Perfect Stream of Life flows through the minds and bodies of these Thy Children; and hold their attention ever fixed on Thee.

Greetings from the Great Host, the Cherubim, and the Deva.

### THE DISCOURSE

Happiness is the great boon every individual is seeking. We find some Orientalists saying that bliss is the ultimate state. It is only another expression for Happiness, but is not nearly so potent to the Western mind. To the Western mind Happiness is God in Action. To be conscious of seeking Happiness is to be conscious of seeking God.

No permanent Happiness is ever attained except through the adoration of God, the "Mighty I AM Presence," which is within, above, and around the individual. *Happiness is a powerful alchemy. It is one of the most powerful purifiers of the human thought, feeling, mind, body, aura, and world of the individual.* If the Student but believed and would experiment with himself or herself, he would find that he *can* generate Happiness at will.

For instance, suppose an outer thing draws the attention and causes some phase of unhappiness. Knowing that God, the "Mighty I AM Presence," is the *only Source* of Happiness, then the Student's first move would be to turn the attention to the *Giver of all Happiness*; and thereby he would tune into the *one Source* from which he is certain to receive.

The idea for the individual to follow is that when he feels some kind of disturbance and wants to turn to God, he may do the following and get great help from it: Get up and go through the motions of taking off a garment that one does not want and, as you would hold the discarded garment in your hands, drop it into the Consuming Flame and know that the disturbing element is consumed.

Then fix the attention on God, the "Mighty I AM Presence," with the Joyous Consciousness of *feeling* and *receiving* the Current of Happiness and Peace filling the mind and body. With a little practice in this manner, the Student will soon be able to come to the point where he or she *can* draw this great Happiness consciously and at will.

Every time he does this *consciously*, he will find that he is gaining strength in the accomplishment and will realize truly that he *has* the ability to reach into the Heart of Happiness and there absorb Its Fullness. This practice is always followed by an expansion of consciousness which is its natural result.

The Students or individuals who are inclined to allow personalities or conditions that seem unusually close to them, to disturb them, should watch themselves closely — and instantly, when they find the attention is being fixed on the outer consciousness, withdraw it and fill the person, place, or condition with God, the "Mighty I AM Presence," and declare to themselves: *"I, through my 'I AM Presence,' consciously fill this person, place, or condition with*

*God. Therefore, in my outer consciousness, I posi-
tively know that only the right and perfect action is
taking place there, toward me and for their success
and happiness."*

With many individuals the love of family holds
their attention entirely too much upon the outer appearances; and when they allow this to be done, they
but intensify the things that they do not want. If
parents will take this attitude toward their children,
*"There is no personality acting in that one; there is
only God in Action!"* then they are doing the greatest
thing in their power to help their children. At first, it
may require considerable determination on their
part to switch the current, but it is really no more
difficult than turning the switch of the electric light
in your room or pressing the button.

The reason individuals find it difficult to do this is
because they do not nip disturbing conditions in the
bud. They allow a fierce momentum to get going
and then suddenly become aware they are in distress
—never stopping to consider that they have allowed
this thing to build, when *by standing guard at the
door of conscious creative thought and feeling, they
can check it and stop its action in the beginning with
little effort.*

Again let Me refer to the power of Free Will and
choice. The individual alone is the governor and

chooser of that which he will entertain; and he or she is at all times and forever *"master of this condition now,"* because *this particular activity requires no special state of growth, but can be done successfully by anyone who will sincerely try.* Almost always the admonition to the child starting to school is "If at first you don't succeed — try, try again."

In looking to the Light or toward God, the "Mighty I AM Presence" with sincerity, we cannot fail, because we not only have our own God Power surging forth to our assistance, but there are other Mighty Powers watching all opportunity to help, from whom we do receive unbelievable Assistance.

*Octaves of thought:* I think it well to again refer to the octaves of thought, for these exist within the atmosphere the same as the strata exist within the Earth. I think it may be wise to define to some degree these octaves.

The first We shall mention is the octave of crime, which is the thinnest in spite of all appearances at this time. The second is the octave of hate — considerably thicker. The third is the octave of anger — much thicker. The fourth is the octave of criticism and condemnation — still much thicker. It is the prevalent octave in which a great number of humanity move unknowingly.

From this on up, we begin to enter the Light; and

we find the octave of Toleration, which is the will to give everyone freedom in thought and speech. Then we enter the octave of Joy where we find ourselves rejoicing exceedingly in the recognition of the God Power *in* us. The next is the octave of Pure Love, from which we feel unmistakably the Presence of God, the "Mighty I AM Presence," acting. From this we come into the octave of Perfect Happiness.

Whenever we allow our consciousness—which means our thought, feeling, and spoken word—to dwell on the quality of any one of these octaves, we not only have whatever we have generated of that quality, but we open ourselves to the entire outpouring from that octave upon which we dwell. This means the full accumulation of that quality generated by the mass of mankind—past and present. This exists within the atmosphere above the surface of the Earth, in which all individuals live and move.

This simple illustration will show how necessary it is to govern the thought, feeling, and spoken word and make determined effort to enter into the higher octaves of consciousness. When we do so, we find that through these octaves—from Tolerance on up—there is a condition just like a funnel with the small point down, direct from the Godhead which is constantly pouring Its Presence, Energy, and Substance into these octaves.

All octaves below that of Love are the creations of mankind—not God, the "Mighty I AM Presence." Mankind is the only one who attempts to divide God. God, the "Mighty I AM Presence," never attempts to divide Itself. God is ALL—everywhere present—to everyone who will accept this Fullness of the "Mighty I AM Presence."

There is no use of Students or individuals feeling that they cannot govern the outer form or the periphery of their thought, feeling, and action, which the body is; for I know *positively* that they *can* and *must* do it! And the sooner they *take* the reins, *accept* their God-given Dominion and *use* It, the quicker they will find True Happiness.

Already, the human or outer self has too long been the usurper of God's Power, feeding the individual on husks and weeds when it might hold the attention fixed on God, the "Mighty I AM Presence," and receive the Nectar of Eternal Youth and Life and move in that octave of Perfect Happiness, God's Perfection—the Garden of Paradise.

*Regarding children:* When children have reached the years of maturity, the greatest thing the parents can do is to consciously place these children in God's Hands, which means to release them completely into the Protection and Care of each child's own "Mighty I AM Presence" and enfold them in the Rays of

Light and Love from the Heart of the Electronic Body above the child.

Every time the presence or thought of the child is in evidence, rejoice that God's Full and Perfect Intelligence is acting in his or her thought and feeling, governing perfectly all outer action. This will release the child into the *Presence and Power of Divine Action* in a marvelous manner. The anxiety of the parent to the child is, in ninety percent of the cases, the cause of a wrong action—and especially so from the mother.

This is a tremendous truth that is little understood. The mother, having been the builder of the body of the child—by this I mean furnishing the substance by which the form was built—has made a personal line of contact with the child for that embodiment; and if the mother but knew it, from the enlightened standpoint, she has the power to mold the child into the most wonderful, perfect being or, shall I say, to hold the focus by which the child is molded into the perfect being.

On the other hand, if the mother allows anxiety, which is a subtle form of fear, to constantly govern her, her thought cannot help but go out to the child and may disturb it to the extent that it would cause the child to be a complete failure. The above is an extreme instance when the mother has entirely ungoverned thoughts.

This illustrates the great importance of parents knowing and feeling that the child or children whom they love are *at all times* governed by the Perfect Intelligence of God, the "Mighty I AM Presence." The moment that anxiety or fear attempts to intrude, consume it and replace it with the firm consciousness that *there is only God's Perfect Intelligence acting in and about the child.*

If all the mothers of America could *understand* this wonderful Truth and *live It*, a majestic race would be born from that time on. This is a great Natural Law that has not been understood even among Students to but a small degree. I have known many instances where the intense fear in the parent for the child, drew the child into the very thing they feared, and it is one of the things that has delayed humanity's progress so much. Sometimes the child is sufficiently advanced so that, unknown to the outer, it wards off to a large degree the fear and anxiety of the parents. This is fortunate indeed.

Let it be thoroughly understood that I am in nowise criticizing or condemning the mothers, but I do intensely deplore the lack of understanding of this wonderful and vital point. I presume that Emily Cady understood this point more clearly than any other teacher of the outer world today, and she made a powerful sincere effort to convey this to her readers.

*Prophecies:* There are certain war conditions threatening. Through the Red activity, war would spread all over the World; and Our desire is to avoid the outburst of it before a certain condition can occur. If this can be done, it will do tremendous things to hasten the progress of humanity. Prophecies for centuries have held forth the idea, and it has become racial in the mind of humanity, that the greatest of all wars called the "Armageddon" would take place.

This, We think from the Higher Standpoint, was a great mistake. Humanity has been accepting it, expecting it, and are determined to have it. In the first prophecy of this, it was to convey the thought that it would take place on the invisible plane, without coming into physical action. We hope yet this may be done.

My personal opinion is that a cataclysm, which is inevitable, is preferable to the coming forth into physical action of the so-called Armageddon; for a cataclysm does not release hate, and because of this, it would be much better for humanity. A certain amount of cataclysmic action is inevitable, and it is not desirable that it should be avoided; for it releases certain things and seals certain things — greatly to the benefit and progress of humanity.

It *is possible* under secured Dispensations, for the channel of the cataclysm to be changed or governed. If mankind could understand that *God forever and forever acts through His Messengers* who are attuned to step down His Mighty Current of Force and Activity, then they would know that all cataclysmic or Cosmic conditions may be to some degree, more or less regulated and directed.

*Warning:* Here again let Me express a very sincere warning to the Student. Even knowing the inevitable, he should in nowise dwell upon it, but should every time the thought of such an occurrence comes to the mind, declare, *"There is only God, the 'Mighty I AM Presence,' in action everywhere present."* This becomes his own Armor of Protection.

If certain conditions can be consumed in Chicago in time, much of the progress here may be sustained and preserved. In calling forth the "Mighty I AM Presence" to consume these wrong conditions, *know that you are using the Majestic Forces of the Cherubim and Deva*, which are anchored over Chicago to give protection. This enables the force to pour whenever the thought recurs.

*Notes:* The principle thing in financial demonstration is to be determined in refusing to accept the idea that money or help is not present. Do not let yourself accept that the thing which you wish to use is absent. It only has an appearance of absence. *You can just as easily find ten thousand dollars in your pocket as ten cents.*

*Sending and receiving thought:* In the case of two individuals becoming attuned, in reality they simply both tune into a Cosmic Force and It acts.

There will come a time when a manifestation of the Ascended Masters will be appreciated and great benefit derived from It. It can then be used with splendid effect and in that case would be justifiable.

The intense element of smoking is what we would shun the most, for it opens the door to things we do not even wish to discuss.

*BENEDICTION:* "Mighty I AM Presence!" Mighty Cherubim! Gracious Deva! We give praise and thanks to Thee and the Almighty Ascended Host for Thy Radiation, Thy Love, Thy Patience in bringing forth the great Inner Light of these Loved Ones to serve with Thee. Let all who come under this Instruction receive Thy Great Inner Illumination.

(Reprinted from July 1936 *Voice of the "I AM"*)

# DISCOURSE XVIII

*September 1, 1932*

SAINT GERMAIN

*INVOCATION:* Thou Mighty, Infinite, Masterful Presence, "I AM," Thou Ascended Jesus Christ, the likeness of which is the Master "Presence" within each Son and Daughter of God! We speak to Thee everywhere! Pour forth Thy Radiant Majesty through the mind and Heart, Thou "Mighty I AM Presence"! Let the Temple of God in each one become illumined with Thy Holy Presence, Majestic in Its Conquering Power.

We give praise and greatly rejoice that at last the Mighty Conquering "Presence" is to take Full Command of Thy Manifestation of all created things, and that Peace on Earth, goodwill to man is at last to become realized and be made manifest, man to man. It has come!

## THE DISCOURSE

I wish now to make it clear that you here, and all who come under the Radiation of this Instruction from the Ascended Masters on the "Mighty I AM Presence," are those who have, these many years, come within the Violet Ray. The Ascended Presence of Jesus Christ, which is the "I AM" in each one of you, is steadily taking Full Command.

Ere long the "Great Mystery of Life," which is the "Mighty I AM Presence," will be revealed in the Heart of each one who comes under This Radiation. Let no one be deceived! The great prophecies of the centuries — in fact the end of the prophecies and their fulfillment is at hand; and from the fulfillment of the prophecies, God having spoken through man, will arise the Kingdom of Paradise — of Heaven upon Earth.

The period of the struggle of creation, in the throes of this new birth, will be swift and to some terrible in its mighty manifestation; but know that it will bring in its train Peace, Happiness, and the Light of True Understanding to the mankind remaining, which is sufficient to make everyone rejoice that through the centuries of this great expectancy, the righteous are rewarded and devotion to God in man is bringing its true fruition.

From the passing of the eclipse of yesterday begin the changes of the Great Spectacle, enormous in Its Dispensation. While everything moves forward and will continue to move under Divine Order, yet the closeness of this surging Inner Christ Power—the "Mighty I AM Presence"—is as though impatient to take Its Full Command.

Try to have your Students understand that the very fact of sincerely seeking the Light of God, if sought with sufficient sincerity and intensity, will cause all problems of the outer to be quickly and normally solved. If individuals, finding themselves confronted by problems, would say: *"Mighty God in whom I recognize and feel Thy full Power of Action! Thou 'Mighty I AM Presence'! solve this problem and do it quickly,"* then calmly enter into the stillness, the Silence of that "Mighty I AM Presence" —they would find and soon feel the peace, certainty, and relief from what they feel to be a necessary struggle in the outer to solve the problem.

It is the *feeling* of struggle in the outer self that really *causes* the struggle. To pour forth that mighty love and devotion to God, always Omnipresent, should without effort bring complete relief from all anxiety. To seek God merely to solve a problem but partially opens the Door; but to seek God, the "Mighty I AM Presence," with true sincerity and devotion for the Light of God, would quickly cause all outer problems to be solved in Peace and Harmony, according to the recognition of the "Mighty I AM Presence" in action.

Ask all those to whom you can convey the idea, to be as conscious as their understanding will permit, that they are now held within the Violet Ray, acting under Its beneficent Radiance. Those who can, should visualize this Violet Ray about them, within Its center the qualifying presence of the soft Pink of Divine Love; and no one of great sincerity should need aught else than this to find *all* outer activity conforming to Its Mighty Presence.

To make oneself a true Student of the Light, the individual will hold unwaveringly the full Consciousness of the "Mighty I AM Presence," the Ascended Jesus Christ, as the constant, Invincible, and only acting Presence and Intelligence in one's mind, body, home, and affairs. It is this steadfastness, no matter what the outer appearance seems to be, that most quickly brings the longed-for peace and freedom.

Already upon the mental or invisible plane is spreading the Christ Radiance, likened unto the dawn of a glorious sunrise. Within a few years the Radiance of that Sunrise, which is of the Great Central Sun, will ascend into the Heavens of Its Eternal Dominion. All who hold themselves steady with faith and confidence in this Mighty Light, will find such individual revelations taking place as they cannot possibly conceive of at this time. I want to assure you with positive conviction, that these are not idle words, neither are they prophecy; yet shall you see them fulfilled beyond your fondest hope.

Those who come under this Radiance, with their determination to receive the Light, will find themselves able to say, " *'Mighty Master I AM Presence!' speak to me!"* and they will hear that Inner Voice as clearly and distinctly as you speak to each other. To those who will listen, I want to assure them that the opening of the Sixth Seal, which is at hand, will make the comprehension of these Mighty Inner Truths clear in such a manner that the Student will marvel that he has been on the periphery of this Great Truth so long, without more fully grasping Its true meaning.

Students and individuals should look within themselves and find wherein there have been, unnoticed, subtle things that are binding them. Each one should joyously open his Heart to the Truth that reveals to him the things which need to be remedied.

Any rebellion within the consciousness should be put down as the *great offense against God*, the "Mighty I AM Presence," so that there may be nothing to interfere with the penetrating Rays of this Great Light. As I have tried to impress upon your minds from time to time, it is not a matter of personalities; but it does mean to enter into the Truth and live It. One of the most subtle forms of rebellion in the outer consciousness is concerning our little personal habits that we have formed through the centuries. As you pluck weeds from your garden, so should you pluck these habits from the outer consciousness. Pull them out by the roots that they have naught left by which they may grow again.

It is My great pleasure to put before you a mighty Truth—namely, that those mighty sincere desires of individuals, in some instances where they seem to have been long deferred, may speedily take form, bringing with them their Eternal Blessing—that is, when they are righteous desires. The earnest Student is ere long to know and understand the true meaning of the Words of Jesus, " *'I AM' the Resurrection and the Life."* Each Student should, in feeling him or herself within this Mighty Violet Ray, meditate on this wonderful and mighty Statement, " *'I AM' the Resurrection and the Life now made manifest."*

Those beautiful Souls who have so much loved the flower creation, ferns, and shrubbery, will find such roses and many other flowers new to the Earth appearing from now on, which will have such rare beauty that it will amaze and delight all greatly. At first, they will not be conscious of where these came from, but will find them appearing in the midst of their gardens. They will later find that the seed and presence was projected from other spheres than the Earth.

The lotus and new forms of the lily will come forth with such magnificence, beauty, and fragrance that their very presence will carry a vivifying, Life-giving activity to the ones to whom they come. The marvelous change of the climatic conditions of the atmosphere will enable these flowers to be ever blooming; and the gardener and farmer of the days that are coming will find themselves no longer confronted with the struggle against weeds, as has been heretofore.

New species of grass will come forth that will make your lawns like a velvet rug, and you will no longer be required to listen to the rattle of the lawn mower. That of which I speak will grow to a certain Perfection where it will remain. This is but an intimation of some of the Perfection that will be the joy of every sincere Student of the Light.

Many will see some of this Perfection, but will still find it necessary to go out and change bodies to permit the manifestation of their Eternal Perfection. But they will hasten to return because they will find the Earth so like the Heavenly World as It now exists, that they will not wish to linger There, but will want to get back into real action, as it were. The time has arrived when it is necessary to give forth some idea of this Perfection; for the Students who grasp the idea and begin to visualize that beauty surrounding them, will hasten tremendously its presence in their Life and environment.

A very remarkable thing that but a few will be conscious of, is that the apples of this season will possess an essence in their substance which they have not heretofore had. Some other kinds of fruit will have this but in a lesser degree. They are the peaches, oranges, and tomatoes.

It would be well if for a time, you ate three apples a day. This will throw off the sediment in the body without making it apparent. The more perfect tomatoes of this season have also contained this element that is being radiated forth.

*Question:* "Will the plants of the future be free from vermin?"

*Saint Germain:* Most assuredly. All destructive force, when it reaches a certain point of activity, will destroy itself. To the human or outer, it sometimes seems a long time getting to that point; but it is so and has always been so. *Cosmic Activity tolerates only so long man's inhumanity to man or man's destructive activity to man.*

From this time on, no individual can gain wealth or the renewal of wealth without knowing that *God, the "Mighty I AM Presence," is the full Source, Power, and Intelligence of its production—and God must be given full credit as the only Producing Power.* No human effort without the *Presence and Activity of God* ever amounts to anything. Too long have human beings been the usurpers of that Power; and even in the usurping of that Power, the time has now come when it will no longer be available to them.

Those who want to find peace, rest, and success must feel and, as it were, throw themselves into the Arms of God as a weary child would do to its mother, and there rest in the Activity of that Mighty Inner Presence — the "I AM."

Sanat Kumara's Daughter naturally acts under the Crystal Ray. All of the Ascended Host at intervals work with Jesus. The name "Kumara" is a title, so think of it as an Authority. The Activity of the Kumaras is distinctly different from that of the Masters from the Central Sun. While the Kumaras come under the Activity from the Central Sun, yet Their Service to the Earth is distinctly different. Of all the seven Planets, They are the Ones who offered to take the Earth under Their supervision — under Their wing, so to speak.

As soon as the axis of the Earth is changed, the Kumaras' Work of countless centuries will be practically completed. *There will be a few years in which They will walk and talk with the Students of Light who are truly aware of their "Presence," which will bless the Students untold who receive Their friendly visits. There has never been such an opportunity in the history of the Earth as at present for those who have any inclination to the Light—and even for those who have not—to be raised enormously.*

*This is the first time in the history of the Earth that there has been a resistless, impelling Action of the Christ Force.* Naturally the Silent Watcher would have to be One from the Central Sun whose Activity is independent of the Logos.

Never lose sight of this fact for even a moment: *Wherever we go in consciousness or thought, there we are.* The Student who becomes aware of the Silent Watcher and goes to Him in thought, cannot help but have a response. You can go out to these Great Ones in consciousness and say, "Speak to me." You can demand any constructive thing of your "Mighty I AM Presence," and it will be done.

The changes referred to above will come within the next ten years. Heretofore, long periods for the upbuilding of the new activity have been required. This time, in a few years there will be accomplished what heretofore has required centuries of work—because the mechanical Perfection, for those who still require it, will not be lost as before. Following this, there will come aerial transportation that has never been equaled on Earth. It will be a still more perfect means of conveyance. The speed will hardly be limited, because of the Earth currents that make any speed possible. Atlantis had this to some degree, but it will come in its fullness now. Airplanes will be made so all danger will be eliminated.

*Donald Ballard:* "Where are You going?"

*Saint Germain:* I am going home today. My present Home is in the Alps. In some instances, the Retreats will be changed and are already being transferred from one place to another. This present, coming cataclysm will end the cataclysmic periods of the Earth, because cataclysms only come through the destructive influence of the human and when that is removed, there will be no longer a cause for them.

*Mrs. Ballard:* "What should one do to stop a fire?"

*Saint Germain:* You could call on the God of Fire to consume it, or say, *"I as the Christ, the 'Mighty I AM Presence,' spread My Radiance over it."* Or you can command its obedience and visualize the Pink Light of Divine Love covering it.

*BENEDICTION:* "Mighty I AM Presence" of the combined Ascended Host, Thou Light Eternal! We give thanks for Thy Radiant, Expanding Presence, that Thou art more and more pouring Thyself forth into Thy Manifestation to the Children of God, that Thou dost dissolve all things unlike Thyself and dost release the Pure Activity of the individual self! Even so it is done.


(Reprinted from August 1936 *Voice of the "I AM"*)

# DISCOURSE XIX

*September 5, 1932*

SAINT GERMAIN

*INVOCATION:* Thou Mighty Infinite "Presence," Thou Mighty Wisdom and Conveyor of Life, Thou Mighty Omnipresence of all Manifestation! We give praise and thanks for the Consciousness, the Realization, the Majesty of Thy Presence. We give praise and thanks that We are aware of Thy All-conquering Presence, that Thou art the Active, Manifesting Principle in all We know as Life, that Thou art the only Intelligence acting. All else is but the creation of man and is not of Thee.

Thou Mighty Presence—O Silent Watcher—as Thou dost bless through Thy Wisdom all humanity, We recognize there are those who know Thee, sing to Thee, call to Thee in Thy Majestic Presence. Answer always those who call. Speak Wisdom, Thou Presence! Speak Wisdom, Thou Consuming Power, and answer all who call unto Thee!

Peace and Blessing of the Mighty Host of the Silent Watcher and His Messengers, to thee and thine.

## *DISCOURSE*

Thought is interior speech; and as you converse with each other by words, so may you converse with, demand, and command the Inner "Presence" through thought. Thought can be made a dynamo by which you can charge the body, home, condition, or activity according to the consciousness or understanding you have of its power.

This brings Me to one of the vital points for all Students, and that is to break the habit of thinking out loud. One has but to watch himself to see how often he is unconsciously expressing the thought out loud. This has to be positively overcome before certain Instruction and Information can be given. Why? Because this habit of the human is a lack of controlled energy; if the person is in the possession of secret Information, in an unguarded moment he will reveal It. I wish each one to take him or herself firmly in hand on this particular point. Do not even in the simplest things in your daily activity allow the thought to be expressed in words, as though talking to yourself.

More Students have fallen down on this particular point than any other one thing. A few days of watchful care will entirely overcome such a habit. The outer is but a conglomeration of habits. In the Garment of the Student who has entered the conscious

Path is placed a Cloak of Protection of Thought. In talking to oneself, the worded expression breaks through this Garment of Thought, and the Student wonders why he does not make more progress. It is because he has caused a leak in the Fountain of Wisdom. Thought is truly the Activity of the Soul of the God-man, the bringing into Activity that Mighty Presence of Energy which may be qualified by thought to any Height of Sustaining Power and Intelligence.

It is said that man may not add one cubit to his height by thought. But I say to you that man, by thought, may liberate within himself the Mighty God Power to make his form a giant in strength or stature. The stature of the human form is to a large degree governed by racial thought — the mass thought being that a certain height is the limit of attainment. Yet within a few years in spite of the racial thought, by the increased Power of the Inner Christ Activity, you will find the stature of men increased to the height of six feet four inches and women to that of five feet ten, with symmetry of form in keeping with the height.

Again, let Me call your attention to the Mighty Truth that thought is the wedge of God's Energy released into action. By this, you can see how important it is to become consciously master of your own thought. In this mastery lies full dominion. In conjunction with the mastery of thought must come mastery of the outer activity; for unless we compel the outer to live in harmony with our idealistic thought, it will pull the thought from its Height and degrade it. Why is this so? Because of long centuries of the building of habit. There is nothing hard or difficult about this; it but requires firm attention. If there are weeds in your garden, you give sufficient attention to them till they are pulled out. So it is with the outer activity. You have but to pluck out the weeds, and leave it clear for the Inner Presence and Essence of God.

Let us go a step farther, which may seem a little more subtle and yet is quite as easy, for it is necessary to recognize your thought as the molder of form. If living in the racial thought has permitted or caused the form to express age or infirmity — an inferior expression of that Mighty Energy, then We know that it has the Power to build the form into Beauty and Symmetry, and to build the perfect brain activity for expressing the Highest Intelligence.

It is vitally important for Students to recognize the difference between intellectuality and intelligence. They must understand that the great intellectual development which some acquire and are often so proud of, is but what they have gathered or accumulated from without, and it does not have a firm foundation. However, the opposite of this is God's Mighty Intelligence, which they receive from within. It is the Fountain of Eternal Truth and has at all times an unshakable Foundation. The brain or intellect is but the vehicle that this Mighty Inner Intelligence uses. It may be taught through conscious action to express only this Inner Intelligence. As individuals of Free Will, We choose which shall act for us—the gatherings of the outer intellect or the Mighty Intelligence in Its full Capacity.

The outer or human has a peculiar subtle faculty —borrowed, of course—of using every opportunity to cause a leak in the great Reservoir of Divine Energy. For instance, mankind are condemned for the loss of energy through gratification of the sex pleasure; but I say to you, one may lose it just as easily without the outer gratification, where the thought is allowed to dwell upon the idea. It has been said that thought is the cause of all outer activity. I say to you, "Beware!"—for a picture of the lower desire may be placed before an individual, and the picture will cause the thought to act. This shows the necessity of the control of the vision as well as the thought. The vision is one activity of the attention.

*Important:* In the coming marvelous period we are just entering, there will not be permitted a single negative picture of any kind, which would be in any way suggestive to call forth the lower activity of thought. This is why We have urged so earnestly that no matter how negative a thought or appearance may be, to instantly take the thought, *"There is only the Mighty Inner 'Presence' and Intelligence of God there operating."*

Whenever you are drowsy and wish to be awake and alert say, *"God is here in action! I will be alert!"* When one has had sufficient sleep, one should take a firm stand and dismiss all drowsiness. Say to such a feeling, *" 'I AM' alert and God is here in action!"*

The Inner Vision has the Power of projecting Itself to any distance. Thus you can be consciously present in two places at the same time. The brain is but the vehicle of the Inner Intelligence, provided so that you can have this experience. When mankind misused this Free Will, they drew themselves down into their dense physical bodies. One can be conscious at the center of a place and at the periphery also. This is how We in the Ascended State can use two, three, or four Bodies at one time and cause Them to act according to the necessity of the Divine Operation, and not necessarily at one given point. They may even be at four different points of the compass. In the Arisen State there is but Omnipresence, when One gets to this Height of Consciousness.

Even a seeming state of growth may be set aside when it is seen by the Great Intelligence that, by so doing, the individual can be a valuable Messenger. Therefore, do not let a conviction form in your mind of previous supposed rules of activity—occult activity. There will be certain individuals, known only to the Silent Watcher, whose entire previous creation and activity may be set aside to become an unhampered Messenger. The time will come when, if the outer attempts to intrude itself, certain Radiation will go forth from certain individuals and compel others to see their wrong activities. This again is illustrated in *The Magic Presence.*

*Note:* It may be possible for the Armageddon to be averted by the cataclysmic activity. That is governed by Those far beyond Us.

*Silent Watcher:* The Cosmic Silent Watcher may act only under the Cosmic Demand.

*Sleep:* It is necessary for you to have a certain amount of rest. As you get into the Higher State, you may find that there may be days or weeks while certain activity goes on—for a Messenger is sustained always during any special Activity. The "Presence," during any special Activity, is always Self-sustaining. Sleep is a complete relaxation of the vehicle. Until the atomic structure is unclothed of its density, this seems necessary so that the outer may receive the

Inner Presence and Inner Radiance continuously.

The conscious use of the realization of the Self-sustained Activity, is the unclothing action of the atomic structure. It is very important no matter what the requirement — that is, whenever the Inner Activity is expected to operate — to be strongly and clearly aware that It is always Self-sustained. If we can become fully aware that we are already in the state or condition we wish, we will then have taken the shortcut to the accomplishment. This is the remarkable Power in Vision, to feel ourselves in the state or condition we wish to manifest.

*A question about the Violet Ray:* "What is the specific Activity of the Violet Ray?"

*Saint Germain:* Use It in Its full color, which is Its normal Activity. Each Ray, having Its own dominant, natural Activity, still contains each of the Activities of all the other Rays within Itself.

The first activity of anything is to become conscious that we have the ability, through the Inner "Presence," to do what we desire to do. Without having the consciousness of being consciously able to do a thing, there is no outlet for it to act. To be conscious of a thing, gives it an outlet; and through this it can act.

We may use the Gold, Rose, and Blue Rays as a Cleansing Process after the Consuming Activity of the Violet. In consuming the thought and feeling, when you command as the Christ, the Flame takes on whatever color is needed to balance the Activity. The Inner Intent is the Intelligent God acting, and is the True Motive or Inner Activity.

*The atmospheric condition when an Arisen Master appears:* A few hundred years ago, when an Arisen Master manifested, He many times came with a rumble or hissing sound, from the intensification of the atmospheric condition into which He came. In the Presence of an Arisen Master is an Intense Force. To a large extent, this has been governed in later years; the atmospheric condition of the Earth is much more pliable to the charging by a Great Presence than it was even three hundred years ago, because the vibrations of the Earth itself have been raised, making it more susceptible to the Inner Activity. The great, sudden impact of the great Transcendent Force on the atmospheric structure caused a concussion, rumbling, or a hissing sound, or flashes of Light.

The cause of a cyclone is the impact of the hot and cold atmospheres upon each other. This impact causes a whirling vortex to ensue, and the duration of the cyclone is in accordance with the force of the impact. The impact of one force upon the other starts a whirling action; for there is more or less an activity of passing each other, and this sets up the whirling motion. In the association of any two elements or different rates of vibration, the natural activity in each is to get away from the other.

There are storms caused by vicious intelligences, and that intelligence acts within the storm. [In the story *She* by Rider Haggard, there is an illustration of this.] The Great Law has seen fit to check this activity. In past ages, tremendous things of this kind were done, which were no myth. Any storm can produce freakish things.

*Question:* "Where are You going from here?"

*Saint Germain:* I am going to Washington from here.

In South America on the great heights of the Andes where the railroad goes by, is another gigantic figure of Jesus, high up in the mountains. I assure you that whenever the slightest attention is given by an individual to such things, there is always Response—whether the person be aware of it or not.

*BENEDICTION:* Thou Mighty Silent Watcher, We give praise and thanks for Thy Radiant Presence pouring into mankind, that Thou hast found pleasure in contacting those conscious of Thee, and that Thou hast looked upon this Center with Thy Benevolent Majesty. We give praise and thanks for Thy Omnipresent, Acting Power.

# DISCOURSE XX

*September 8, 1932*

Saint Germain

*INVOCATION:* O Thou Almighty, Majestic "Presence"—Infinite Creator of all there is! Thou Dispenser of Life to all form! Thou Great Giver of Intelligence and Activity to all form! We give praise and thanks eternally for Thy Ever-manifesting Presence perfecting all Creation and drawing it again into the Perfection of Thy Mighty Self. Infinite is Thy Intelligence. Infinite is Thy Strength and Omnipresent Activity. Let the Children of men feel and know this for a certainty, that they may open the Door of their consciousness and receive Thy Mighty Strength of Life, Intelligence, and Health, manifesting Thy Perfection now. Greetings from the Silent Watcher and from the Great Arisen Host to you all.

## THE DISCOURSE

As we recognize the Mighty Messengers of God and Their continual pouring forth of that Supreme Essence and Energy, so do we know there is but one process by which They pour This forth, and that is *thought*. Thought is one of the mightiest means of Creation; and as it creates the smallest thing, so does it create the greatest. This will illustrate how necessary it is that mankind should govern their thought and feeling. Thus, they would govern all outer activity in harmonious production.

As we contemplate the use of thought, finding that it will create the simplest thing, then we must know that it will create all things. When it does not seem to do so, it is because unknown there is lurking doubt or fear. All sincere Students should analyze their thinking consciously, and see if there is doubt or fear or anything negative. If there is, find out what it is, and then proceed to eradicate it from the consciousness at once. As Students of a Mighty Truth, if we have become aware of the slightest fundamental Principles of Life, then we have learned that our thought, when held on the awareness of God's acting Presence, creates constructively with a majestic dominion.

It is so unwise for one of God's Children to sit in judgment upon another; for to do so, means that we are not exercising the full confidence in the Mighty Presence of God anchored in the Heart of every one of His Creations. For each one to talk to the Mighty "Presence" in the other, asking It to perform and manifest Its Great Perfection in all outer activity, would be the ideal way and the correct usage of our thought, and would bring forth greater results than the outer can possibly comprehend.

*To Mrs. Ballard:* I have just arrived from a very definite association with France. The French are one of the nationalities to which I have dealt out the strongest force, yet I am not a Frenchman. The World is My Home. To create good is My Religion. After We have raised the body, We have forgotten there is nationality or personality. Nationality represents to a nation what personality does to the individuality. We but see where the Great Light is needed most and endeavor to radiate It there — if not through speech, then through thought that carries the Mighty Radiance to Its destination.

If Students will not take the necessary time to be still and feel the Great "God Presence" filling their minds and bodies, then they have no one but themselves to blame if they do not receive as much of the "God Presence" as they desire. The Student, having Free Will, through determination will always have whatever time is needed to still the outer and receive the Majestic Splendor of that Mighty Inner "Presence."

If one who has been physically laboring feels the necessity of rest, that one should first sit in a comfortable position and, entering into the joyous recognition of God's Mighty Energy, feel It flowing through his or her mind and body like a Mighty Cleansing Stream. If the Students would practice this simple exercise daily, they would shortly come to the place where they could call forth a Mighty Stream, so that in three to five minutes they would feel entirely refreshed.

The assertion may sound absurd to you, but I assure you the sense of growing tired from outer activity is but a lack of joy in the thing you are doing. It may be something from racial thought or something from an inharmonious condition in the individual. Knowing the body of itself cannot grow tired, then we know the sense of being tired is a lack of joy or harmony in the consciousness somewhere. Naturally then, the first thing to do would be to still the outer and feel that Mighty Joy and Peace filling the mind and body full to overflowing, just like you would see a pail of water full to overflowing; and that Radiation would spread to those who need It. The first requisite to the use of Exhaustless Energy is a continuous happy, harmonious state of consciousness.

Most individuals have a mistaken idea that this Mighty Energy of God is something they have to pump into activity or pull out from somewhere, but I assure you It is likened unto an artesian well. When you have struck the level of the water, it requires no coaxing to rush to the surface in a continuous stream. So it is, when we enter deep enough into the Consciousness of the Mighty Presence of God: we tap that Mighty Fountain of Energy, and we do not have to coax It at all. It rushes forth like water bursting through a dam; and we may direct It wheresoever we will, for that is our Divine Birthright and Privilege.

*Desire:* It seems necessary again to put forth the Mighty Consciousness that desire is the Mighty Activity of God — the motive power, as it were, by which the wings of thought carry it forth into productivity. There cannot, I assure you, be a single thing from the lowest to the highest without desire back of it; for desire is the power of the Soul trying to find expression. There are those who will tell you they have many wrong desires, but I assure you it is only because of a lack of control of the Free Will. Any full-grown human being knows the difference between letting the Energy go out into constructive or destructive channels and, therefore, can easily choose where It shall go.

It is so vitally important for the Student to have the correct understanding about desire. So much has been said — and falsely — about the Supreme Ideal being to kill out desire. To do so would be but to come into a state of apathy where you would open

yourselves to all the destructive forces there are!
When you have a constructive desire backed by its
twin sister, determination, knowing that each is but
an Attribute of God in Action, that moment you
have loosed the mightiest Power for and of Achievement.

Every experience that comes to the individual
serves a double purpose: first, to turn the attention
to the only Creative Source, God; second, to make
the individual aware that resting in that Supreme
Consciousness is the solution, instantly at hand, of
whatever needs to be known. We do not receive it by
throwing up our hands and screaming for help, but
by taking the opposite stand and becoming so still
and quiet in the outer that there is not a ripple of
disturbance upon our consciousness. Then we will
quickly find a solution to whatsoever is required.

In understanding the mighty power of creative
thought—and thought is always creating one thing
or another—one cannot help but at once feel a great
freedom, for no one can prevent us thinking what we
will. In the sincere recognition of the Great Intelligent God Self, we remove the possibility or power of
the outer self of anyone to say or do anything that
would be disturbing to us; for so long as we are
resting in this Supreme "Presence," Its Mighty Radiance or Energy is constantly carrying with It the

Consuming Power of all outer disturbance.

It is only when we allow the attention to begin to be held on an expression of the outer, that we give it power to disturb us. To instantly take the stand that there is no personality—there is only God in Action—would prevent the "stinger" of ignorance from finding a landing place. Ignorance, like a hornet, always wants to use its stinger, but does not know where to find a landing spot unless you disturb its nest. And no one will knowingly do that if he knows the nature of a hornet. Divine Love is the original nature within every human being. Inharmonious feeling or activity is but misapplied energy trying to gain something by force, which it can only have permanently through kindly, harmonious action.

*Love:* If individuals could only recognize that God's Love is the natural motive power of their being, they would see at once how their attempt to use energy not qualified by this Mighty Power of Divine Love, must necessarily bring them just the opposite results from those which they wish. Therefore, let all sincerely open the Doorway into all expression—into all activity; and we will find our world transformed and moving within an Armor of Protection where only Light, Peace, and Harmony reign.

The first simple essential to the constant use of the mighty constructive energy is to determine to move within the Sacred, Charmed Radiance of your Mighty "God Presence." We have often seen, through many lesser experiences, that we can do what we are sufficiently determined to do. In the determination to use the constructive power, which is God in Action, then we have loosed the mightiest Power in the Universe to act in our behalf.

The moment we become conscious of God's Energy, we set It into motion. In Its Infinite state, It is static. Consciously directed, It is dynamic. This is the reason for the demand for the *conscious* use of understanding. This is the subtle point where individuals fall into a state of apathy, and it should be avoided as you would a poisonous serpent.

*The Silent Watcher:* The Radiation of the Silent Watcher takes on the Quality that is needed at the point to which It is sent.

*To Mrs. Ballard:* Let Me assure you, you have accomplished a wonderful thing in receiving these Words to the song, "The Silent Watcher." It has drawn His Current of Mighty Creative Power; and He will use as His Messengers, the Gracious Cherubim and Deva. For the Classwork, the Silent Watcher pours His Radiation direct. His Radiation at the home of Mrs. _____ was both Consuming and Energizing.

*The Divine Flame:* To some natures the sense of

warmth is disastrous to keeping awake. The mentality should become alert and awake with very great vividness as the consciousness is held more and more on the Divine Flame. Do not let the seeming lack of anything find a resting place in your consciousness. Take your stand that you are free right now, and feel it. When we love God enough, it causes us to enter into the "Presence" sufficiently so that whatever we wish is forthcoming.

*The most important Service:* The first and most important service of every human being should be his or her devotion to the Great Light.

The reason there are so many more masculine than feminine Masters in the physical octave, is because it is very much more difficult for the feminine to shut out the ever-present sense of curiosity, which comes from the fact that they constantly live more in the feeling element. Therefore, it requires a much firmer hand and much greater determination to govern that, than what the masculine has to contend with. This, however, must be completely governed by the feminine element before real, permanent progress will bless their efforts.

Occasionally there is one using a feminine body who, although delicate and refined, possesses enough of the positive masculine consciousness to govern the otherwise uncontrolled feeling. These individuals become great feminine Masters; and it is worth all the effort anyone using the feminine form can make, to attain it.

Before fifteen years have passed, you will find the World smaller than ever. Television and the right aerial transportation will make the World like a great audience chamber. It is much nearer than most people suspect. Things are steadily progressing. There are at least forty percent more settled, normal conditions in the business world than six months ago. That is a very great gain. The price of things will be maintained at a much more normal balance.

The stock market is a disgrace to humanity when in it, one man who wants revenge against another, has a certain means of gratifying it. The entire system of everything will be changed in such a manner that individuals will be protected; and the selfish element of the big fish wanting to swallow up the little ones, will have made them so sick that they will not wish to try it again.

I would suggest that you keep up the sending of Peace and Freedom to all humanity; for where there are sincere individuals, it can be utilized to very great advantage. You cannot come into contact with the Radiation of these Great Ones and not have these things manifest.

*BENEDICTION:* Thou Mighty Presence! O Silent

Watcher! We give praise and thanks for Thy Mighty Radiation, for the Light and Wisdom flowing forth like Rays—a Mighty River reaching out and enfolding all who are sincerely reaching to the Light, making them Thy Center of Radiation. Strengthen Thy Great and Loving Messengers to go forth, conquering victoriously in the spreading of the Great Light to mankind. Draw to them Those who can give them Great Light and the Students who can receive that Light. Thy Love enfolds and Thy Peace sustains all mankind forever.

# DISCOURSE XXI

*September 12, 1932*

SAINT GERMAIN

*INVOCATION:* O Mighty "Presence," We give praise and thanks, and rejoice in Thy Mighty Radiant Presence — that Thou hast come forth to clothe America in Thy Mighty Radiant Presence and shed Thy Splendor o'er humanity. We rejoice that the cycles of time have moved forward, and this has enabled Thee to come forth from Thy Secret Chamber in the Temple of Light. Mighty One, in the Majesty of Thy Splendor, Peace, and Power, look into the Hearts of those who sincerely look to the Light. Strengthen them! Give them courage! Enable them through Thee, Mighty God within, to hasten and come forth and be the Messengers of the Mighty God Light. Speak to the Hearts of the Children of Light. Strengthen them to stand and be sustained in Thy Great Splendor.

I bring you Greetings from the Great Angelic Being who has been caused to look upon this humble effort to give forth Light, and who extends personal Greetings to you all.

## THE DISCOURSE

With the entrance of each great cycle there come certain presiding Beings of great import. You will know this Presence as a Being of Great Majesty, Power, and Light — through whom, at the height of all civilizations, has come the Power of Precipitation of Jewels of all kinds and of liquid Gold. This Presence represents the All-Seeing Eye to the Earth. Your request to know more of the Great Beings has been granted. It was through the Action of this Great Being and One from the Jade Temple whom you shall later know, that there was caused to come into form the "Jade of Ahbor." Another such twin of the "Great Jade" will appear in America. It will be publicly known of at a later period. This entirely depends upon humanity — how soon they will turn, and where, to the Great Light.

Beloved Children of the Light! Fix firmly in your minds, all of you, fix within your consciousness that the Mighty Presence of God in and about you is the only Intelligence, Presence, and Power governing the Universe. With this staunch, firm recognition and adherence to the Great Light, there is no Height you may not reach, no great service you may not render through this great Acknowledgment! It is your right to command and compel the outer to accept the full significance and magnificence of this great opportunity.

You have reached a point where you can compel the outer obedience to the Great Light. And at this time, I say for the benefit of all Students who will take their stand and determine to serve the Great Light to the fullest of their ability, that they will receive a Mighty Sustaining Power, aside from their own effort to hold themselves steady in the Great Light! It is so foolish and childish for anyone who is sincerely interested in serving the Light to say that he cannot control his thought, feeling, and spoken word; for where the sincere effort is maintained, the greatest Assistance is sure to be given.

I congratulate you most sincerely in having drawn the Radiance and Attention that is now and will henceforth be continuously manifest to you. It is important to compel the feeling to accept the Great Truth of this, that it may not at any time waver and wonder how this Majestic Truth can be true. The accumulated good of centuries of effort is being stirred into activity in many sincere individuals who are determined to serve the Light.

The words "I can't" or "have not" are to be forever wiped out of the vocabulary of the earnest Students of the Light! When they once know the Mighty Living

Presence of God is the Life Energy flowing through their minds and bodies, they must know that there is no longer any excuse for the use of such words. These words are simply concoctions of the outer human self to try to justify itself when, by its own acts, it has shut the Door of Light to itself and its world.

Having arrived at the full stature of manhood in Christ, we should be able to put away all childishness of doubts and fears, and leap into the Arms of that Majestic Conquering "Presence" in the Life of every individual, and accept Its full Manifesting Presence. The unwavering acceptance of the Limitless Presence and Activity of God, manifest in your outer experience, is the Miracle-working Power, and has long been waiting to pour forth Its great Abundance into your use.

All human doubts and fears are fast being consumed and eliminated; and that makes it possible for this great Inner Abundance to rush forth like a mighty stream, bearing in Its Embrace the fullness of the "God Presence" into your use and experience. Consciously give full power to this feeling with all the joy at your Command: "How true and wonderful it is now, in my Life and world!"

This is an illustration of what tremendous things can be done, and what it means where one will make the sincere effort to maintain peace and harmony in the consciousness. If each of these individuals can and will feel the full import of this great Truth, marvels can take place in their experience — and *will* take place with this full acceptance. This is not a wish to intrude anything upon the Free Will of the individual, but is a statement of facts and the Eternal Truth concerning these Higher Manifestations. When We find that there are those Children of God who will accept, in confidence, small trusts, then in time they will find themselves recipients of great and mighty trusts. No one knows his or her strength until Sacred Trusts are given into his or her keeping.

*Liquid Gold:* Liquid Gold is sometimes precipitated for its emanation in Healing. It is very like quicksilver, only of gold; and its structure is very similar. As a rule in contacting this denser vibratory action, it always contains a shade of jade green. In its Higher Activity the green is hardly perceptible, and in this state it takes on a shade of light rose in place of the green. Whenever intense Raising Activity takes place, there is always this observation, yet rarely is the individual conscious of it.

I trust you can, each of you, feel this wonderful Radiation about you, filling you with this joyous feeling and adoration of that Great Light. Try to feel yourself a great fountain of It, pouring forth all the time, knowing that there is but the one Mighty

Intelligence, "Presence," and Power of God acting through your mind and body. *"I rejoice that 'I AM' free, forever free, from every limitation of the outer world."*

*Use for pain in the head: "This thing is nothing! Therefore, there is nothing in me that can accept it. I know there is only the Mighty Presence of God acting in my mind and body. Therefore, in God's Activity there is no pain or disturbance."* Many times if you begin to contemplate a source — something causing a disturbance — it gives it power. Sometimes it is necessary to know, but now we must take the stand not to accept anything of the negative. Give it no attention, therefore no power. The attention sometimes gives a thing power that we are not aware of. Lest one fall into a mistaken attitude, if there seems any unusual activity at any time, take the consciousness, *"All of God's Activity within my mind and body is perfectly natural and normal."* This balances the outer and avoids the misinterpretation of that which is really a blessing, into becoming a disturbance.

*Use this often: "There is only God in Action in my mind and body!"* If there is a wrong thought about an experience, you neutralize or requalify it, and thus you lose its Blessing. In all of God's Activity in the Raising Process, it is impossible for It to contain any disturbing element unless the outer mind misinterprets it and requalifies it as a disturbance.

*Remember:* To avoid this, one should at all times, in feeling an unusual vibration within the mind or body, take this attitude about it: *"How beautiful and glorious this feeling is, for I know it is God's Great Presence at work within me!"* When you begin to consciously use this Energy of God within you, you are qualifying It in some manner all the time. So it behooves the Student to awaken to the fact that he cannot take anything for granted, for he is supposed to qualify whatever passes through the consciousness. This is why We suggested some time ago the use of a Mighty Truth: *"There is no personality! There is only God in Action!"* At that time We did not think it wise to give this explanation.

*Question by Mrs. Ballard:* "The idea conveyed by mythology that there were, at one time on this Earth, any such beings as the Cyclops is a mistake, is it not?"

*Saint Germain:* At no time have there ever been beings with the Spirit of God within them, with but a single eye. Such an idea was a distorted view concerning the former state of those beings who still retained the full function of the Third Eye or Inner Sight, like the X ray. The All-Seeing Eye is the right conception of this state.

There was a time when those which are known

today as the pineal gland and pituitary body were one. They were the All-Seeing Eye. The skull or brain structure, which was of denser substance, was in nowise any obstruction to the use and activity of this Inner Eye that really looks in all directions. To the All-Seeing Eye, no form is an obstruction to the Vision. At all times the All-Seeing Eye has the form of an eye as you know it today. The greatly dimmed activity of that function, even today, causes you to sense a presence behind you as well as ahead of you.

At this previous time as the Soul drew into denser form, it required the activity of an arc, as it were, by which the two activities in conjunction stepped down the activity of this Inner Vision. This sparking broke the image of the vision, the same as an arc breaks up the current; and instead of a steady flow, it was in intermittent jumps. This causes the present intermittent activity. This became necessary as the outer form reached a certain density not wise to explain at present. If there could be a continual flow or connection of Light between the pituitary body and the pineal gland, we could see everywhere and through all things at all times. This is really the Inner Sight! This would be the same activity as when they were one—or in other words, unite them into their oneness again. When one can visualize the two as the All-Seeing Eye within, wonders might take place.

*The child with the X-ray eyes:* In this case the pulsation between the pineal gland and the pituitary body has become so frequent that the flow is almost continuous. In all forms where the Power of the All-Seeing Eye is used, the shape of the human eye is retained as we have it today. In any thought of this, think of it always as the All-Seeing Eye, complete, in the top of the head—taking the place of the pineal gland and pituitary body, or as having these two organs within it.

In this Eye within is the Perfect, Eternal Sight of Almighty God. A mental picture of anything, with this power back of it, must be propelled into outer form because it is God Power moving through it. This is how the images we see with our physical eyes are registered on the brain. Therefore, make your pictures within. Your eyes are the camera of the Soul. The activity of the vision in the mind acts just the opposite of the activity of the eyes, or physical sight.

The secret of manifesting things into the world without, is in using the Spiritual Power to take this picture. Then the Great Silence precipitates it into form through the visualized picture. Through the activity of visualizing, you print the form or picture upon the Great Silence; and the Great Silence, which is the greatest Power in the Universe, propels it into outer expression and experience. Now you can understand how impossible it is for a picture registered on the Inner Silence *not* to come forth.

It is the business of the intellect and will, to hold the picture steady until the impression is taken by the Great Silence. If it is not held steady, the result is the same as if you moved your camera while taking an outer picture in ordinary photography. This is the Power of true Precipitation.

You do have all power within your consciousness to mold your mind and body or any of its parts or attributes into anything you wish. Meditate on this incessantly. Contemplate this matter of vision often enough to set it in mind — in action — and use it. This release of Truth and conviction is tremendous! Never forget it! Use it more and more all the time. This is the Inner Power that knows Its own and is waiting to do these things for you all the time. A tremendous Power has been generated here today. This conviction you now have, you can use with great power.

*Warning:* After I have given the Explanation of the Law and you have received the Inner Power and conviction, do not discuss it, for you scatter the Power which would accomplish the full Manifestation. You have the vision, the power, and the ability to apply this. Now do it! The Power of Precipitation is one of the mightiest activities of this wonderful

Presence who is radiating to you today. You have been shown how Precipitation through vision takes place. Use: *"Great 'Presence,' completely and entirely reveal this Activity of Visualization and Precipitation into physical form to me now. Teach me all about This, and see that I always use It to fulfill the Divine Plan, to the Glory of God and the Blessing and Service of all His Creation."*

*BENEDICTION:* Thou Mighty "Presence," We leap forth to Thee in great devotion and recognition of Thy Presence with Us. We know, feel, and have the full conviction of Thy Presence eternally with Us, and that Thou wilt teach us the fullness of Thy Activity manifest in form.

# DISCOURSE XXII

*September 15, 1932*

SAINT GERMAIN

*INVOCATION:* Thou beauteous, overshadowing "Presence," as Thou hast come from the Secret Channel wilt Thou touch that Secret Place in the Soul, in the Heart of each of God's Children. Strengthen, encourage, and lift them into the Embrace of their own God Self within, who through the centuries in Infinite Patience has watched over them, sustaining the outer form, which is gaining its great freedom from personal limitation.

We give praise and thanks for Thy overshadowing Presence in America, governing everyone on Its surface and holding Thy Children in Its Embrace — making each one Thy great Messenger, to heal, to prosper their own world and America. O Thou Precious Jewel on the brow of the Great "God Presence," may Thy scintillating, prismatic colors shine forth like the Mighty Rainbow of Promise in the sky, filling the Children of men, causing them to stand to the Light eternally and be bathed in Thy Lifting Radiance.

Greetings from the Great Host, from the Great Radiant Presence, Cyclopea, watching in His Mighty Transcendent Power, lightening the burdens that otherwise would rest upon some of the Children of men in the coming readjustment of things.

## THE DISCOURSE

Oh, that individuals might center within and feel that Great "Presence" — the Giver, the Preserver, the Solver of all things; that they might consciously anchor within that Great "Presence" with such certainty and assurance that doubts and fears could not beset them, enabling them to steadily rise in that Great Eternal Victory which must sometime, somewhere be accomplished.

I thank you exceedingly for the two pieces of music that are most useful to Us for the attunement to the Great Height and for America whom We wish to bless. I would be pleased if those who are in complete Harmony with you, would hold that the individual who can best serve the Christ alone will be made President of the Nation.

As this Work goes forward, We wish each individual to feel his or her part in the Great Victorious Activity — that they are as important to the working out of things in the Universe as the petals of a rose are to its beauty. There is constant opportunity for those who have a joyous attitude toward this Effort, to be channels of Outpouring of this Mighty Radiation.

The Student who is sincere and is with great intensity reaching out to the Light, need never worry about making direct contact with the Ascended Masters; *for it is not the Student alone who seeks the Master, but truly the Master who seeks the Student* because there is always great need of Messengers of the Great Host of Light, who are staunch, trustworthy, and willing to serve. Such may never doubt for one moment their eventual contact with the Visible Presence of that Great Ascended Host, not only with one but many.

We have no desire to intrude this Work which We know to be a Mighty Truth, upon anyone; and anyone who cannot feel within the Heart the Truth that We give forth to strengthen and to cast out doubt and fear, should either wait or seek other channels with which they can feel perfect accord and harmony.

This Work shall go forward without interruption or interference and, as a Mighty Magnet, will draw to Itself Its own. No one can go beyond the point where their understanding carries them. Our only Desire is to bless, to strengthen, to enlighten all who come within This Radiation. We seek no one who does not come with a joyous willingness to put aside all personal things and rejoice in the great activity of the Mighty Inner Presence of God, of which We are but the Messengers.

Those whom We contact through the Radiation are always free, and they alone must choose whom they shall serve. How strange it is that enlightened Students will discuss individuals and Activities of the Truth, and allow doubts and fears to beset them, which sooner or later make a barrier between them and the great Beauty of the Light they might so graciously enjoy.

We or Our Messengers have no thought or feeling of criticism toward the individual who cannot come with Us; and to all such, We give Our Great Love and Blessing. But this Work We are doing must stand free from criticism, fear, and doubt, in order that what We are accomplishing may be done with the least outlay of energy and without unnecessary strain upon Our Messengers. Students, through the drawing power of the outer, allow themselves to discuss this Presentation of the Truth with those who know nothing about It, many times causing an obstruction to their own beautiful acceptance of this expression of the Light. Each should know for the other, that there is only the Mighty Presence of God in Action in each one—in their speech, thought, and action; then they would avoid the subtle pitfalls that are but breeders of disturbances. *"God in them! show them the Light unerringly!"*

You might also know concerning the political activity, that *"God's Mighty Love governs every channel of activity in this coming election, and God's Mighty Presence silences all outer action and expression, allowing the Truth to manifest in Its fullness."* Cyclopea especially wishes to utilize It as the Outpouring of that Mighty Radiance to America and to Her people. Calmly and silently know that the Mighty Radiance is spread over the entire Country, touching all Hearts and raising them into the receptivity of that Mighty Radiance. There has been an attempt to turn the tide against Justice, and We trust this will prevent it.

*BENEDICTION:* We give praise and thanks for the endless stream of dazzling Light enfolding this Activity and each individual in It. This Radiance goes out to those who are looking to this Presentation for the Light, and We enfold in that Great Intelligence all who can receive It.

# DISCOURSE XXIII

*September 19, 1932*

SAINT GERMAIN

*INVOCATION:* O Mighty Luminous "Presence," from out Thy Secret Place Thy Radiance shines brighter and brighter; and as Thou dost encompass America and humanity in Thy great Loving Presence of Light, so We give praise and thanks for the Privilege of being Thy Messengers to carry forth Thy Thought, Thy Work, and Thy Word into the various parts of the Earth, there to be blest by Thy Beneficent Presence.

O Mighty Host of Light, as Messengers of that one Supreme Power, We give praise and thanks for Thy Ministering Presence to ourselves and all mankind. From out Thy Great Wisdom comes the solution of all things. From out Thy Great Light comes the great Consciousness that opens humanity's consciousness and is the Great "Presence," Self-sustained forever.

Greetings and Love from the Great Host for establishing conditions in which They delight. There is a difference between musical peace and ordinary peace, as We term it. This Music is Harmony of the Spheres and carries much higher and farther than other activities, except where the thought is sent — propelled — by conscious dynamic force.

### THE DISCOURSE

The old seeming myths and legends were far more true than the humanity of today are willing to acknowledge. The Gods and Goddesses of the olden times were greatly enlightened Beings whom the humanity of that period looked upon as too superior in Wisdom and Light to ever dream of becoming like Them. However, the Children of Light today, through the Inner, Propelling Power of the Individualized Christ Force, realize that there is no height, no matter how great, that one may not reach — and there, be forever Self-sustained.

*Reminder:* I wish again to call your attention to what was given last week on visualization and ask that you read it daily so that you get the true conception of visualizing. Contemplate it as often as you can, for I am aware that the door of your consciousness is opening to receive the full use and understanding of its mighty power. The quickening of the understanding established last week is leavening the whole loaf, as it were; and with your cooperative, conscious effort in contemplation of its great activity, you will come more and more into its tremendous use and possibilities.

The Activity of the Light is consciously drawn about you, and the Radiation that goes forth is reaching a point of saturation, chemically speaking, at which Its Radiance runs over, as it were, like a pail of water filled to overflowing—this becomes a Fountain of ever-pouring Light, Illumination, Substance, and Power governed by Wisdom enfolded in Its cloak of Divine Love. Thus is there no uncertain activity. Be conscious of the overflowing Substance and Power flowing forth to wherever you are conscious of a need. This will become so tangible and so potent in Its operative Power, that ere long It will stand ready and dart forth like a Ray of Light wherever there is a Call or Demand.

It is well to be aware that there is no limit to this Outpouring. You arrive at the point of consciousness where this Mighty Power surges forth to fulfill the Demand, without contacting your physical body. Why? Because the consciousness reaches a Height of the Self-sustaining "Presence" where it is, can be, and will be more and more directed from the Electronic Body—which will maintain this Outpouring in calm poise and peace. The only activity required is to fix the attention upon that which is consciously known to be needed.

Aside from this, be aware that from the Height of the Electronic Activity the Work is constantly going on, and being consciously directed from the Great Master "Presence" within. This is preparation and a very important step to the outer and Inner becoming one. When there is sufficient calm, peaceful preparation, the Wisdom flows like a gently flowing stream, carrying with It a conviction and radiance not possible in any other way.

*Daily work until the tenth of October:* Spend at least three to five minutes every night until the tenth of October, making your clearest visualization of the All-Seeing Eye—which is the highest, yet normal means of causing the pineal gland and pituitary body to act in Perfect Balance. This will naturally cause other centers of the body to act in harmonious accord with It. In this manner Divine Love and Wisdom are naturally caused to act upon the lower centers, raising their activity in a manner and grace not otherwise possible. This will bring splendid results.

Each Student should for five minutes in perfect quiet sometime during the day, claim the full power of perception and its full activity in his or her Life and world. This will enable everyone to have Insight and Foresight concerning their activity and affairs, which are activities that all Students need and really crave very much. One should contemplate that one has right now the full God Power of Projection and Precipitation, and the Power of molding and manifesting the Inner Substance into whatever form is desired. This may be applied by all of you.

Here is a Secret not conceived of or known except in the Retreats, which is an exact opposite of what is ordinarily understood from the general activity of the outer: When the Inner has raised the outer to a certain point of recognition, the outer begins to rejoice exceedingly in its cooperative action. From this point on, the Conscious Effort to hold fast to the joyous desire to act within the Magic Circle, makes it far easier than I can explain to you in words. Several of you are reaching this point, for which I rejoice with you.

*Warning:* Each one of you should take a firm determined stand that no thought of criticism, judgment, or condemnation should at any time find lodgment in your consciousness. " *'I AM' enfolded in the Mantle of the Master Christ; therefore I maintain my thought, feeling, and words free from all criticism and judgment.* " This maintained will open Doors of wonderful Light and Activity. With this, take the stand that when you have done the best you can for an individual through Instruction or

Radiation or both, you place that one in God's Hands and insist that your outer self remain free from the contemplation of the subject. This will give a Power, Activity, and Use of the Inner "Presence" that will many times amaze you.

*Hints to the Group:* We feel greatly encouraged over the unusual Harmony manifested within the individuals yesterday. If this great loving, joyous feeling of one Student to another and to their Instruction is maintained, wonders may occur at any time in their midst. Several have sought the Visible Presence of one or more of the Ascended Host. This attitude maintained might enable such a desire to be fulfilled for the Group. If each can enter joyously into the acceptance of this Idea, it will be well indeed.

In contemplating the use of the True Vision, let each one demand of his or her Inner Self, unwavering conviction in Its use; for when the Vision has placed the picture desired within the Great Silence, it is positively certain to be propelled forth into visible form, the moment it has registered there with sufficient clearness. Do not have any consideration except to know that the picture is placed within the Great Silence—firm and clear; and you will not need to be concerned when it will manifest, because the Law of the Great Silence is to propel it forward into visible form the moment it is registered.

As a rule, the Student endeavoring to place the visioned picture within, immediately begins wondering if it really got there. This questioning prevents the clearness of the picture striking the Inner plate or Great Silence. When the picture is made, the only office of the outer is to know positively that it is registered in its full and perfect clearness — and then rest in that. The wish has gone forth. Know that it has gone forth and brings its visible action.

*The disappearance of animals from Earth:* One of the most amazing things perhaps, in all manifestation, is the tremendous power that the love of an individual has, to lift the consciousness of an animal, as is so beautifully illustrated in *Unveiled Mysteries.* It is a beautiful illustration of how the intense love of mankind for animals will soon remove all animals from the outer expression.

*Metempsychosis:* There was a time in the progress of humanity when the conscious division of the constructive and destructive use of the Inner Power and Energy began. Through the power of black magic, or misuse of the One Energy, sometimes a Soul was driven from its body by another; and a body of an animal was built up, and the Soul was compelled to use it. It was from this condition that the legend of the transmigration of Souls came. There has only been one period through the centuries at which this occurred. The Ascended Host consumed and dispelled this activity forever. But the memory, which has never been erased in an etheric record, still lingers; and now and then an individual having contacted this record, keeps alive the idea that should long ago have been forgotten.

*Dominion over the body:* People can, *if they will only realize it,* talk to the organs or parts of the physical body just like they would to a child from whom they wished obedience. They can say, *"Now you get into perfect normal activity and see that you maintain it!"* During the time that the Life is maintained within the form, there are innumerable little workers whose duty it is to rebuild the atomic structure of the form and maintain it in perfect order. Again one can say to that part of the Life activity, *"See that my body is supple, perfect in form, and beautiful; that my hair, eyes, and every part of me glows with the Light of the Inner Activity."*

The fact and Eternal Truth is that the consciousness is absolute master of every activity of the body and can mold it into perfect activity and form. The only reason those who know this do not get their manifestations is because they do not stay on the job. If a disobedient child were destroying something beautiful and valuable in your home, you would certainly put a stop to it. The time has come for you to do permanent work on your bodies.

The work of repairing and perfecting the body is done through the Electron. Say to the intelligent workers in your entire body, *"Get to work and see that every particle of this structure is replaced with God's Perfection."* Do this especially at night before going to sleep. Realize that you are setting to work intelligent Beings who obey you. The consciousness must be impressed upon the workers that the Perfection is permanent. The Electron is a Focus of Perfect Energy from which the workers draw their Perfection. Instead of knowing that everything we place within the body is God's Pure Substance, most of us have the idea that some of God's Substance can be harmful. The idea that any of God's Substance is naturally harmful and inharmonious to man is absolute nonsense.

*To meat eaters:* The reason that flesh food does not belong in the human body is because there is a certain animal quality in the natural structure of the flesh and this automatically acts from its own trained environment of activity.

*Question:* "What causes the change in desire for food?"

*Saint Germain:* It comes through the raising of the consciousness, and this quickens the activity of the atomic workers.

*Very important:* The force field around the Electron is naturally Perfection. The force field between the positive and negative atoms may be so charged with the force of the Electron, that it maintains a constant constructive activity. This is done by the Conscious Activity of the Thought through the Vision. The province of the Conscious Activity and the right use of Its power is to qualify this force field between the atoms with the Perfection of the Electron. The nature of the little workers is to keep Perfection. A good Affirmation is, *"See that this is renewed and maintained in its perfect activity."*

*Remember always:* The human mind will revert back to imperfection unless you keep a death-like grip upon it until it makes full union with the Golden Flame. Take your stand! Know you have within you the Mighty Master "Presence," and tell It to see that you are sustained in the constant activity of Perfection. You must consciously give quality and permanency of the quality to the atomic structure if Perfection is to be maintained without interruption. Command often: *"I speak to you, the conscious workers of the constructive process! See that Perfection is created and maintained in every function of all my bodies."*

*Germs:* There is no germ of any disease, except what the conscious mind creates. The medical profession call this activity germs.

*Phagocytes:* These little workers are constructive by nature and are placed in the body to maintain Perfection; but the discord in the thought and feeling — if allowed to express in the consciousness of the individual — compels them into other than their natural activity or work.

*For healing more quickly:* Whenever you visualize the Golden Light acting, qualify It with Infinite Intelligence, and command these little workers to create and maintain Perfection in the mind and body. This adds a tremendous element to the Healing Activity, which is the natural action of this Golden Light. In the Light is an Intelligent Activity. When This is directed by the Conscious Command, It sets in motion tremendous Power of the Christ. Get the full realization of this fact at all times, so that you will know that this consciousness always acts according to your Demand. Instead of allowing these little workers in the body to accept destructive suggestions, by your Conscious Command you keep them obedient to their own natural perfect activity. Whenever you hold the vision on Healing, be sure to qualify it in this way with the Conscious Command.

By the use of the Conscious Command as the Christ, we transcend the Law of Growth. The Law of Growth is only in the outer activity. There was a time when birth came through the Power of the Inner Vision creating the full form as desired by the Masters within. This is the same Power that is used today by the Ascended Host who project forms for Their own use. The Ascended Beings at this time, unless a number of Activities are required at once, usually take Their own Body for the Work. If three or four activities are required at the same time, They project that many forms through which the Energy is to act.

The Law of Growth is only a concept of the human mind that accepts the limitation of and the concept of time. The Ascended Host can send or project a form just as easily as a thought. The instantaneous action of the desire creates the form by the thought —for Their Thought Creation is instantaneous. If you wish to project your thought to a distance, you have but to clothe it with your picture. To make a form tangible to the outer senses, it must be clothed in the atomic structure.

The transportation of a body by Levitation is a much lower action than the Dissolving and Reassembling of it at a distance. The latter is a much more rapid process. The manner of transporting the objects from the Temple at Mitla to the Royal Teton, was by the Disassembling Process. This was the Method used for all in the Retreat except the Portraits. In the case of the Portraits, We did not wish to interfere with the cohesive structure as it had been previously established, for reasons not explainable now. In passing through solid objects, things are disassembled and reassembled on the other side. In this way we keep the Inner blueprint intact and reassemble the article again according to that Perfect Pattern.

*BENEDICTION:* Thou Mighty Infinite "Presence," We give praise and thanks for the clearness of thought and understanding today, and that Thy Mighty Intelligence is now acting in the minds and bodies of these Thy Students, Eternally Sustained in Its fullness and activity.

# DISCOURSE XXIV

*September 22, 1932*

SAINT GERMAIN

*INVOCATION:* By the Sign of the Heart and Head, which is Thy Symbol of Love and Light, We greet Thee, O Silent Watcher. In the depths of Thy Great Peace and Silence, We reach forth and receive Thy Mighty Radiance filling Our lives, homes, and worlds with the Conquering Activity of Thy Mighty Presence. Out of the Fullness of Thy Active Presence comes the quickening cooperative action of the outer and Inner Life into Full Expression in the Life of each one.

We offer eternal praise and thanks for that eternal contact with Thee, and that We know that evermore Thy Master Presence is giving of Itself every assistance required in maintaining the Perfect Contact with the Mighty God Self in each, so that We may live, move, and reap the Great Reward of Eternal Peace, Eternal Vigilance — eternally receiving that Great Light more strongly each day in Our lives.

### THE DISCOURSE

Within the consciousness of each one is that Eternal Vigilance on guard which warns the outer to refrain from anything that would create destructive activity, if the individual will only listen to its prompting. For any Student to yield and lower himself to vicious gossip is a violent retarding process to his or her growth. It matters not what may seem to be the appearance, no one shall sit in judgment upon another. They who yield to such childishness open their doors wide to forces more destructive than the boa constrictor of the jungle, or the tiger that would tear them to pieces. That would but destroy the outer form, while gossip, criticism, and condemnation build within the mental bodies that destructive element which takes them many embodiments to rid themselves of.

If Students receiving these Instructions cannot resist the vicious onslaught of these accumulated elements, they should withdraw from the Classes until such time as they can conquer themselves and are able to send love, peace, harmony, and goodwill to one another. Students should understand, in entering into the Conscious Action or Stream of Life, that they are or have entered into the sifting process, wherein they either rise on the Wings of Eternal Love or fall by the wayside and are swallowed up by the dragon of the outer forces.

The Students who have entered upon the Conscious Path and wish to proceed and be blest by that Wondrous and Mighty Light anchored in the Heart of each one, should turn from criticism and judgment as they would from a poisonous serpent that would strike the poison of death into their flesh. The Students should understand that in allowing themselves to fall into this most undesirable habit, they but injure themselves. They cannot harm another who is filled with love toward everyone and all things, because the Consciousness of the Activity of Divine Love in the individual's Life builds a Mighty Armor of Protection that naught of the outer can penetrate—for God is Love and always protects His own.

The Students who have had difficulty in controlling their thought and feeling harmoniously should understand that when they have entered This Radiation every faculty of their beings is quickened tremendously. Therefore, they are more sensitive to the undesirable as well as to the good and desirable. But I cannot stress too strongly that everyone, having Free Will, has the power to govern and control how they shall think and feel. They should at all times keep this Truth before themselves.

The one who spreads gossip, true or untrue, not

only injures him or herself, but often shuts the door for those who unfortunately accept the gossip and dwell upon it. So, anyone who yields to it should understand how far-reaching it is in the injury they do themselves and their acquaintances. The conscious pouring forth of Divine Love into all situations will enable anyone who is addicted to such a habit, to find quick and complete release from all such conditions.

I rejoice exceedingly when one with great Inner Strength is able to resist and refuse the acceptance of subtly destructive suggestions, and to stand firmly with and in the Mighty Presence of his or her Glorious God Self. Keep it up, Dear Ones, and you shall hear the Bells of Freedom, of Liberty, chiming to you in the Great Rhythm of Eternal Light.

*The Classes:* We see and know the beauty of Soul of everyone in your Classes. They have been brought to you through the Mighty Presence of their own Divine Selves. It makes the Heart ache to think that anyone might shut the Door to the Great Blessings and Light on their threshold. However:

> God alone is Great
> And holds within His Hands Eternal Grace.
> And as we stand strong and firm,
> We will see God face to face.

A volume is really in these four lines. When it is said

that "We see God face to face," it is an actual fact that hundreds of staunch ones have experienced; for the God governing the Universe is One and the same as your own Mighty Master God Self.

It is time that sincere Students should understand that their own Mighty God Self, ever pouring Its Energy into their use, is the "He" who created all Worlds and brought all Substance into form. I admit that this is a stupendous thought, but it is true; and they who will meditate upon this simple yet Mighty Truth will find the Highest Door of their Consciousness opened, and they will be able to accept and utilize this *Eternal Truth*. It is the unfortunate teaching through the centuries that has caused mankind to look away into some distant place for this Mighty Presence of God.

It is a misstatement that no one may look upon the Face of God and live; for I know hundreds of Students of the Light who have seen their own God Self with the same clearness and assurance with which you look upon each other in your outer experience. *The God Self in you is the same God that is at the Heart, at the Helm of the Universe.* The pity is that Students think or feel this too stupendous a Truth to be realized in their individual lives; but I assure you that according to the intensity with which they recognize this Truth, anyone with unwavering determination may see the Radiant Face of that Mighty "God Presence." These statements are neither myth nor imagination, but tremendous Truths that the Students can grasp, comprehend, and utilize with Everlasting Blessings in their outer experience.

It seems strange that many Students who have studied, and to a large degree earnestly and sincerely, do not awaken to the fact that self-correction of the outer is the simple, yet Mighty Activity that must be used. *The outer self of each one must be conquered, and there is no escaping this fact. This is what Mastery means and there is no Mastery for anyone without it.* Those who are earnest and determined will naturally receive Great Assistance, but those who will not make the sincere effort will find the Door shut to their further progress. May God bless them and show them the Way.

The Help that has been focused upon the Earth of late, through the effort of Cyclopea—the Silent Watcher—the Cherubim and Devas, and the Highest Influence from each of the Seven Planets of this System, has been caused to focus that Power upon the Earth, making the Earth as the hub of a wheel, symbolically. There are those in your Classes who will see this Activity, and I call the attention to it because it will help those who may see it.

*The province of the Students of Light:* The real province of the sincere Student of Light is to be able to know of the outer destructive forces generated by mankind, to look into them and see there, *active*, the Mighty Presence of God, consuming everything unlike that Glorious "Presence." He or she must be absolutely fearless about destructive forces or what seem to be disastrous reports.

*Your visualization:* As the sunrise of a brilliant morning absorbs, as it were, the morning dew or mist, so will the visualized Presence of God, held firm within what seem to be destructive conditions, have a similar effect. Thus, it is seen what tremendous Blessings to humanity may be brought out of seeming chaos; for it should be at all times remembered that the outer is but the changing, shifting quicksand of man's outer creation. Therefore it has no permanency, and it is the Privilege of the Students to become wonderful Messengers of the Light. Some will say, "But how do I find time to do this with all the outer activity about me?" I say to you that anyone who will try to, will find day by day more leisure time in which to do this great Service.

*Newspapers:* If every newspaper in the land would start printing in great letters across the first page of their newspaper, "Rejoice! God's Loving Peace and Prosperity are here!"—in seven to ten days, the Transformation would be complete. However, I believe that the *Tribune* of Chicago and the *Denver Post* may be yet inspired to some such fearless activity, and they would be amazed and encouraged how fast humanity would fall in line with the idea.

*The All-Seeing Eye:* The All-Seeing Eye is the Presence, the Radiance, and Activity of the Mighty God Self and is really the Silent Watcher.

*Learn always to reverse at once everything that is contrary to the Perfect Activity.* Nip it in the bud and say, *"This is not true; I do have what is Perfect!"*

Life, Love, Light, and God are One and the same. These are just different expressions for the same Activity.

There is really never any drawing-down activity onto the physical plane. The only Activity is always a Raising of the physical by the Inner "Presence" to Itself. All activity of the outer comes from the Energy given by the Inner "Presence"; and therefore, the proof stands before you that all is a Raising Process, and what seems to be the activity of the outer is in reality the exact reverse of the Real Process: by the Inner "Presence" projecting down Its Energy, the outer is set into motion in a spiral-like Activity that draws it Upward.

As the atoms form the body or outer form of the

individual, so do individuals form the atoms in the Great Body of America or of the Christ. Individuals are atoms in the body of a government or empire.

*Gandhi:* Gandhi is entirely on the Love Ray.

*Encouragement:* There are times when encouragement is absolutely necessary and imperative, for it lifts and carries over in certain activities. At other times all is withdrawn, and the Soul is left alone to prove its own strength and reveal the impulses still within it. Know always in all trials, *"There is only God in Action in me, and 'I AM' sustained by that through all trials."* Know also, *"There is only God in Action in all my affairs, and 'I AM' abundantly supplied and sustained by that!"*

*BENEDICTION:* Thou Mighty Radiance of the Crystal Light! As Thou hast manifested through Thy Wondrous Messengers, so do We give praise and thanks for Thy Eternally Sustaining Power, ever pouring Its Radiance and Presence into Our lives, world, homes, and experience. Into the Heart of every sincere Student, let Its Sustaining Power flow.

# DISCOURSE XXV

*September 26, 1932*

SAINT GERMAIN

*INVOCATION:* Thou Great Star of Light and Love! We are filled with great Rejoicing that Thou dost again, after so long a time, project Thy penetrating Rays of Light upon the Earth. Through Thy Mighty Quality and Power will the Mighty Light of the Christ, the "Mighty I AM Presence," find entrance into the Hearts of humanity, holding Thy Anchorage there, so that Thou mayest hold and sustain the attention until the Fullness of the Christ finds Dominion in the Hearts of the Children of Earth. We give praise with great Rejoicing, that the Mighty Creator of all things and Thou have seen fit to shed Thy added Radiance to the Children of Earth once again.

I bring you Greetings from new Friends. I bring you Greetings and Hope from the new Radiance. I bring you Love and Greetings from the Great Host of Light always.

## THE DISCOURSE

One of the first things that all Students should fix firmly in their consciousness is the Truth that they cannot divest their thought, feeling, and spoken word of their creative quality and power. This, firmly held before the consciousness of individuals, will do much and will explain why it is so important that they control their thought, feeling, and spoken word.

Mankind through the centuries has made the great mistake of focusing the attention upon the human accumulation instead of the Principle of Life within the individual—the "Mighty I AM Presence," which each one really is. Even from outer observation, all who stop to think seriously must know that this Principle of Life, which we see everywhere manifest, is Eternal and is the Activity of God—the Creator of all things visible and invisible. Therefore, that Principle of Life within us is *One* in Quality and Power with the Creator of the Universe. Again, may I remind you that you have for your conscious use *all* the Qualities, Power, and Activity of the "Mighty I AM Presence"—the Godhead.

Then *never* again forget your limitless possibilities. God, the "Mighty I AM Presence," thought that which you see, into form. That same mighty inherent Quality is in your thought today. It is your privilege to use this inherent Quality in creating Mighty Perfection in your individual world. In this Mighty Creative Presence and Principle is that Eternal, Omnipresent Opulence. By Opulence I mean money, Love, Light—the Eternal Power of Activity, the Peace and Harmony of the same Quality and Fullness that are in the "Mighty I AM Presence" or Heart of the Great and Mighty Silence, the Great Central Sun.

With your Mighty Power of Free Will, there is naught in the Universe as authority for what you shall think, feel, or say—or naught to prevent you thinking, feeling, and saying—but yourself. Then awake! O Students of Light! into the use—the conscious use—of this Mighty Power naturally inherent within you.

There is a great mistake that mankind has long made; and in bringing it to your attention, I wish to indelibly impress it upon your consciousness. It is this: through observation, the outer consciousness of mankind has observed things—creation—from the standpoint of growth, when to the Student of Light, it should be looked upon from the standpoint of Expansion. Correct understanding will wipe out of the consciousness this inhibition or idea of growth. Growth, to the outer sense, requires a short or long period of time, according to one's comprehension or attitude toward it.

The idea of Expansion will enable the individual consciousness to feel its liberty and freedom more quickly—*now*. It is our privilege to express and use the completed, perfected form of the object, article, or substance which we wish to use. This consciousness of Expansion comes about through the recognition of the Expansion of the "Mighty I AM Presence" —the *All-powerful Principle of Life*—which animates, governs, and directs the outer form.

It is time now that individuals erase from their consciousness the idea of growth, which signifies more or less time, and enter into their God-given Freedom through Expansion. Then live, move, and *be* that Fullness and Freedom in and of all things, which is everyone's birthright!

I will make a personal effort with whoever contacts this Instruction, to assist all to erase from their consciousness the idea of time and growth, and to enter into the Expansion of that Great God Self, the "Mighty I AM Presence"—wherein all they require or wish to bring into expression and use is already within their worlds, awaiting their ability to open the Door and call It forth. Everyone whom this Instruction reaches will have the ability to do this, with the assistance which will be given. We must come to the point where the outer and the Inner are *One*; and the recognition of this Expansion of the God Self, the "Mighty I AM Presence," is that *Oneness* — or rather the true *Oneness* will come through this recognition.

There are a few individuals who have recognized in a small way that they now live and move in their own perfected worlds. The idea or consciousness that there seems to have been a past, that there is a present and possibly a future, has led the outer activity of the mind deep into the consciousness of growth. The realization of the Expansion of the "Mighty I AM Presence" in the individual will enable all who understand this, to enter in and use this Perfect Kingdom with enormously greater speed and certainty. The Students will be able to enter more fully into Its great Use.

Beloved Students, try to realize with great intensity that this Energy which you are using every day even to lift your hand, has inherent within It the Mighty Intelligence, Power, and Activity of God — the "Mighty I AM Presence"! Not having been aware of this tremendous Truth, you have unknowingly requalified and charged It with all kinds of limitation.

Another of the great mistakes that individuals make is in taking entirely too seriously the outer appearance and, by that seriousness, giving it certain power. For instance: a seeming accident happens and the great crowd of minds says, "Oh, that is awful," when it may be the best thing on Earth for the individual and all connected with him. The ideal of control would be for one to take the attitude of always living in the poised restraint of the emotions. To the one who will do this, it will be a tremendous blessing.

*The Love Star:* Today for the first time in two thousand years, the Love Star, created and sent forth to this System of Worlds by the Intelligence of the Great Central Sun, has begun to shed the Rays of Its Radiance upon the Earth; and today, the first Rays have touched the Earth.

This Radiance was present at the birth of Jesus and during His Ministry, and withdrew at His Ascension. It has again appeared and will remain for more than a thousand years. I assure you this is an Activity the astronomers will not detect with their physical instruments, nor will there be any astrological records of It whatsoever; but It is nonetheless tangible in spite of that.

Before, when this Star appeared, It held principally or dominant in Its Outpouring the Element of Love. This time Its Radiance holds in Perfect Balance Love, Wisdom, and Power; and this is a part of the explanation of why We have said repeatedly that the Christ Power will almost seem to intrude Itself, but only because of the quickening activity that has entered and will enter into the individual's consciousness.

This is why those who misuse the Great Energy and Privilege they possess will find a tremendously quick reaction. This will become so noticeable that even the newspapers will speak of it, let alone the individual's recognition of it.

This which I am voicing to you today is broadcast o'er the land by Our secret radio of The Middle Way. Why do I say, "The Middle Way"? Because it holds in firm grasp the balance of the outer and Inner Activities.

All who grasp and make sincere effort to utilize this, will find amazing experiences awaiting them — not for the gratification of any curiosity but for great rejoicing that they at last recognize the Use of their Supreme Heritage. Those who can recognize that which has been stated relating to the Love Star and who meditate on Its Mighty Presence, will find themselves at times as though held in the Embrace of a Great Individualized Being. This will bring such a Consciousness and sustaining uplift that many times they will scarcely feel their feet touching the ground.

Do not misunderstand this statement. This will not make them less equal to cope with problems of experience, but rather the opposite; for this added

Sustaining Power will often be of great astonishment to them. This is but a small illustration of how tremendously the Power from the Love Star can be used to solve all things and make that solving permanent. Furthermore, when the conscious Power of Divine Love is used to counteract and consume that which is unlike Itself, It is the Mighty Presence and Power of God acting.

*Mrs. Ballard:* "I saw the Rays from a Star focused upon me, while resting. What was the Outpouring?"

*Saint Germain:* It was a Mighty Reality and no mistake, because of the Incoming of this Love Star; for you had been holding fast to the Activity of Divine Love.

*Mrs. Ballard:* "Why did I receive such a strong Current and Outpouring of Light when I was calling for Divine Love as the Healing Action, and also when I used the phrase, 'Venus, the Love Planet'?"

*Saint Germain:* Because you had been holding your attention upon the High Power of Venus, or the Great One who has charge of Venus. He already knew of this and was cognizant of the Love Star.

For more than fifty years the Planets above the Earth have been conscious of the Love Star, because Venus is the Conscious Assistance of the Power of Divine Love to the Earth. This directing activity will affect many, many things. It will cause a dissolving of the discordant element on this Earth, and in no way will it intensify the disturbing reactions.

There are those who pray, beg, and plead with God, when all about them is all His Opulence to pour forth into their midst. They do not receive It because they, in their ignorance, do not know that it requires conscious preparation. Those who do not consciously prepare themselves will only receive a fragmentary part of that which those receive who have made the preparation.

*Mrs. Ballard:* "What is the color of the Outpouring from the Love Star?"

*Saint Germain:* The Activity of Its Light is almost like the play of a searchlight, on the lens of which you place various colors. Its own individual color is liquid or molten gold, but the Controlling Intelligence is constantly qualifying It according to the demand in the various localities.

This is the first time Its Activity has ever played over all the Earth. Two thousand years ago, Its Outpouring only included Judea, of which Bethlehem was the central focus.

*Mrs. Ballard:* "Will this Star pour out a still greater Power at Christmas?"

*Saint Germain:* Yes, because the consciousness of mankind is raised at Christmas, and this, through long activity, has caused humanity to feel Peace and a Radiance pouring through them at this time of the year. So it is a tremendous opportunity to utilize any additional force that is at hand.

*Mrs. Ballard:* "Was this the Star that led the three Wise Men?"

*Saint Germain:* No. The Star visible to the Wise Men was a Radiance from the Divine Self of Jesus, which at the moment of the Ascension caught up the outer form in Its Eternal Embrace.

*Mrs. Ballard:* "Was Jesus' Manifestation to this Earth only a small part of His Work?"

*Saint Germain:* I think it well to give a much needed explanation, which your question brings out. According to the intensity of the individualization of every Great Master Presence, does that One draw from the Great Fountainhead all the Power, Authority, Wisdom, Love, and Activity that is required at a given point of action.

The question might readily be asked, "Why did the Star appear to the Wise Men, so-called?" Because in a previous Dispensation, They had been Associate Messengers of the Light and Their recognition was indispensable to the Work that was to be done.

You will notice that there were three Wise Men and Jesus made four, which was the Cosmic "Squaring of the Circle" for that Dispensation to the Earth.

This enabled that Activity to take place without interruption.

There are those questioning minds that will say, "If God is *All* and Omnipresent, why are these Manifestations mentioned of added assistance?" Because of all the fears, doubts, and unbeliefs of the outer shell, built up by humanity. Thus they would have greatly delayed the Cosmic Progress intended, by the use of their own Free Will. This Cosmic Progress must and does at all times come through on Cosmic Schedule.

An individual in his upward progress without the Assistance of an Ascended Master, may poke along indefinitely not knowing that he may reach up and, through his "Mighty I AM Presence," contact those Great Ascended Masters who have won the Eternal Victory over the Earth and its activity.

One of the great Privileges and Provinces of the Ascended Host is to aid those who discover Their Presence, and the great masses of humanity who do not. But those who do not have the certain Knowledge of Their Presence, can only receive a fractional part of that which comes to those who do have certain Conscious Knowledge of Their Existence and Assistance to the Earth.

Again, let Me call the attention of the Students to the Truth that in looking to an Ascended Master for

Assistance, it is exactly the same as looking to your own "Mighty I AM Presence"—except that Those who have passed this way and attained full Victory and Mastery, have the Conscious Knowledge of that Victory with which to assist the one not yet Ascended.

The following is a point very little understood, which so often creates fear on the part of the Student concerning the Masters of Light: The Masters at no time intrude Themselves in any way upon the individual, but do respond in a wonderful manner when the attention of the Student is focused upon Them. Their entire Work with every individual, be he a conscious Student or not, is to help him *feel* a much quicker and more personal contact with his own "Mighty I AM Presence," his Divine Master.

When a Student is fortunate enough to have Conscious Knowledge of the Ascended Masters of Light and Wisdom, and works with Them in Conscious Cooperation, it enables him or her to easily accomplish in one, two, or three embodiments what might otherwise take twelve or more to attain. Then is it not worth all the conscious effort and determination it takes to hold fast to these Great Ones and Their Teaching, to keep from poking along and waiting for the Great Cosmic Activity to prod you along and propel you forward to the place where you should be?

There has been a great lull in the activity of occult students in the last forty years because many in the outer groups and some on the Inner did not receive the visible manifestation and expression they desired. The principle reason is because, as stated in *Unveiled Mysteries,* many activities of the old order of the occult world are being transcended, and that which is transcended becomes obsolete.

This may be a shock and cause a roar on the part of some occult students, so it is up to Me to catch the roar and consume it; but that does not alter the Truth. The Dispensation or cycle which required the secrecy of occultism is closing, and we no longer need that activity. There was so much fear within the old activity, and the progress of the age was such that it required the closest secrecy concerning certain phrases of the Law; and even then, there were those who would turn and misuse them.

In the use of the Rays of Light, you have the Power to reveal without the danger of misuse, because that which the Light and the Figure of the Christ show anyone, is for the Blessing and Service of Light and Love. The Light reveals only that for which the individual is ready; and any other idea concerning It is but the imagination of the outer activity of the mind and is not the Truth from the "Mighty I AM Presence." The Light only recognizes

Perfection and cares nothing about the outer, foolish activity. As the Students hold themselves more and more in the Activity of the "Mighty I AM Presence," they *must* express more and more of Its Perfection.

I would add that you consciously place within the Radiance of this Great Love Star, every discordant thing in your consciousness and world. Be conscious that every discordant activity — individual and otherwise — is caught within the embrace of this Mighty Radiance, until every discordant activity is erased and consumed. Every time the thought of such activity comes to your mind, know that it is consumed and that you do not have to repeat it. Give your attention and adoration to the Secret Love Star and the Ascended Masters, for you cannot help but get a response — always.

Often the feeling of a band or something tight around the forehead is a Cap of Crystal, Golden Light. It is placed upon the head of an individual to hold steady a certain activity of the Radiance from that one's own "Mighty I AM Presence." At a certain point in everyone's Expansion of the Light, this is always done.

*BENEDICTION:* "Mighty I AM Presence," Creator and Precipitator of all manifestation, We give praise and thanks that Thy Mighty Invincible Law is now in full and complete operation in the consciousness of these, Thy Messengers, and that all feel the full import of this. Hold each in Thy Mighty Embrace until he or she experiences the full conscious use of Thy Love, Wisdom, and Power.

(Reprinted from June 1936 *Voice of the "I AM"*)

# DISCOURSE XXVI

*September 29, 1932*

SAINT GERMAIN

*INVOCATION:* O Mighty Majestic "Presence"! Thou Mighty Active Principle of God, forever endeavoring to press forward into action, into expression! Thou Wondrous "Presence," Thou Eternal Light and Boundless Wisdom, We give praise and thanks that We now and forever firmly recognize Thy All-pervading Presence in Our minds, worlds, homes, and affairs. No matter what appears, let Us stand firm in the recognition of Thy Wondrous Presence.

I bring Greetings from the Great Host to you all.

## THE DISCOURSE

At the Door of the Consciousness of every individual should be engraved forever the words, *"Be yourself."* I mean by that, dependent alone upon that Mighty "God Presence" in you. No matter how wonderful the experience that comes through another channel, train the outer self to look to that Deeper and Truer Self from whom will come that Great and Deeper Expression, satisfying every demand. The disturbance in the outer self and world, in at least seventy-five percent of the cases, is due to consciously or unconsciously receiving and acting upon the suggestions of others.

If we observe and feel the "God Presence" within, impelling us to action, we can use suggestion many times to get advantage instead of being used by it. This reference is to the outer conditions as one moves about the world in his daily vocation. Of course, this does not apply to True Instruction; for Truth is not suggestion, and we are supposed to apply Truth conscientiously and sincerely.

*No adverse conditions:* Be it now and forever understood that to the Student or individual who has become aware of his Mighty "God Presence" within and enfolding him, there is no such thing as an adverse condition, no matter what the appearance seems to be. No matter what the appearance of anything seems to be, with the attention fixed upon this recognition, it is impossible for anything but good to come out of every condition. You can see at once how impossible it would be for God to make a condition that would affect Himself adversely. No Student can attain and maintain his or her freedom from limitation without recognizing and applying this simple yet Mighty Truth.

It is so childish and foolish for one, in the recognition of this Mighty "Presence," to continue to give power and authority to outer things. After Students have entered the Conscious Path, they should understand that they must keep the conscious guard for their protection, their defense, their deliverance — and know positively that God in them is the one and only Directing Intelligence.

*Unwelcome thoughts:* It is useless for the sincere Student to say, think, or feel that he cannot govern his thought and feeling. I assure you that at first it does take determined watchfulness; but it must be done, and there is no getting away from it. If strangers began to open the door and pass through one's home unannounced and unwelcome, I am sure it would not be long until the individual locked the door and, if necessary, placed a notice outside that only those invited might enter, and none without being announced. The same principle can be applied in governing the mental world or world of thought. We can place the sign outside of the Magic Circle of our active Life, just as tangibly as we can place it on the outside of the door of our home.

The Student can say with full authority: *"God! My Mighty 'Presence,' surround me with Thy Mighty Magic Circle, that naught unlike Thee may find entrance at any time. See that this is sustained without a break anywhere; and with Thy Invincible Power and Wisdom, enable me to govern and qualify eternally all thought and outer action with Thy Full Dominion."*

*Warning—watch this:* My Heart yearns for the Illumination of the Student who keeps voicing day after day, week after week: "How am I to govern my thought? Why don't these affairs come into shape as I want them to? Why doesn't everything change about as it should?" Dear Student, let Me say this: Because in the first place, you have built it, created it in your world. In the second place, every time you say "why," "when," "where," "how," or "what," you are giving power to the old outer momentum.

*Stop! Look! Listen!:* Use the motto that has come forth in your outer expression in the signs on your streets— *"Stop! Look! Listen!"*—every time you are tempted to make a negative statement, or admit things less than Perfection.

*Saint Germain's Promise of Help:* I tell you that everyone receiving these Instructions who will take their determined stand to govern their thought, feeling, and action, will be given boundless Help and Assistance. Of course, you will understand that thought, feeling, and action are but three expressions of the one force. Instead of allowing yourself to lament over your seeming inability to master the outer, use that energy to conquer the condition by giving it the quality you need for the solution of your problem. Say: *"By the Power of God in me, I can acquire full mastery and do it now; and I positively refuse to give power to outside conditions, persons, places, things, or activities. I have learned to know that there is only God in my Life, my mind, my body, my home, my world, and my affairs."*

In your schoolwork as a child — and most people have had their difficulty with mathematics — when adding up a column of figures, if you did not give your full attention to it, your answer would undoubtedly be incorrect. If your answer was wrong about three times in succession, your attention would be called to the fact in unmistakable terms.

So it is necessary for you to take this same determined stand, no matter what the appearances seem to be. If necessary, silently shout to yourself within: *"I stand firm! There is only God in Action in everything with which I am concerned."* I am grateful indeed that some are understanding the great necessity for self-correction and are determined to succeed. All who do this will find themselves steadily forging ahead and, time after time, have proof of this Mighty Active "Presence." This will shortly give them all the faith and courage in the world to place their feet on the neck of the outer self and hold it always subject and obedient to this Mighty Inner God Self.

Oh, Beloved Students, why waver and wobble around any longer? Brace up! Tighten your belt! Face and conquer this outer self *now*, and go forth in that blazing Light that will draw around you to the point where you will not have to be concerned about the outer activity, by the Law of your Inner Being. It draws to you all Harmonious Action, Love, Light, and Wisdom, which you will joyously send forth like a Mighty River of Light, pouring Its Presence and Radiance over those blessed ones who have not yet gained the Fullness of the Victory.

*The quick Victory:* The Student who wishes to gain a quick Victory over the outer must cease lamenting the outer conditions because, in doing this, he is unknowingly giving power to the outer appearance that is holding him in the very condition that he does not want or like. Again let Me remind you, give no power to anything but God in your mind, in your business, in your home, in your world!

I trust after this explanation, that no Student will be so unfaithful to his or her own "God Presence," as to fail to recognize Its Action in everything he or she desires. The Radiance of God be with you all and help you to do this.

*Phagocytes:* It will not be long until the Students of this Work will settle down to commanding the little workers in every part of the body, to enable them to do wonderful things in the body. It might be a very powerful expression to use: *"Mighty Master Self within! Command and direct the little inner workers of my mind and body, and see that they produce Perfection in every organ and part; and see that this constant, constructive process is sustained and maintained continuously."*

*Renewal of the body:* With this Understanding it should be very easy for each one to experience *complete renewal* of the body within a year. The fact is that there is no imperfection in any part or organ of the body, which you have not placed there through your thought. Therefore, you see how easy it is to stop that wrong thought-activity and change it into building the Perfection, instead of the imperfection.

Now here we come to a most vital point: the natural, inherent tendency within the Life Principle of the Individual is Perfection, therefore constructive. So when you turn your attention to the Constructive Principle, you return again to the building of that Perfection which you had left — and therefore have a hundred-to-one odds in your favor for Its accomplishment.

*Resentment:* Where there is resentment toward a

person, place, condition, or thing in the outer, you are but heaping fuel on the fire and binding it closer to you. The minute people resent, criticize, condemn, hate, or blame, they are creating with tremendous speed more of the same thing to chain them that much longer in the bedraggled garments of limitation.

*Gossip—this is an urgent warning:* I am going to say something to you, Dear Students, that to some may be shocking, but it must be said: Could individuals see how they clothe themselves when they wallow in vicious or unkind thought or gossip, they would scream for deliverance; for I assure you, I would not stain the Consciousness of your Great "God Presence" by attempting to voice such a description. If we really know that there is only God in Action in all our outer experience, we can readily see how perfectly ridiculous it is for anyone to permit the outer to lament about anything.

*For the real Student:* The blessed Student who sincerely wants to know the Truth, will face it—no matter what it is—buckle on his or her Armor of that Mighty "God Presence" within, and conquer it, no matter how fierce the battle. But if at all points he keeps himself reminded that there is only God in Action here all the time, he will find the otherwise great struggle diminished a thousandfold.

*For yourselves and the Students who receive this Instruction:* Everything is tending to draw the Power to the topmost Center, and a wise Statement is: *"God! the 'Mighty I AM Presence'! See that the energy in my body is perfectly balanced throughout my mind and body."*

*"God! See that this person, place, or condition is harmonious in action here, right now!" "Arise and go to the Father,"* is marvelous for business conditions especially.

*For a sense of tiredness: "I absorb the Mighty Presence and Energy of my God Self, and it expresses as alertness, joy, and abundant activity in my outer Life and affairs!" "God is my Energy, expressing in my outer activity right now!"*

*All supply:* If there seems to be an absence of anything, God in you is the Creator and Supplier of it. Instantly give the Command that God does supply it abundantly right now.

*Mrs. Ballard:* "Just an idea that came to me, to say: 'This is God's Diamond Palace! Now you get back to your right place in the Universe and be quick about it.' "

*To Donald:* It is so important to watch your feelings. I had a Student once who had a similar condition, and I told him to say to everything, "God bless you." He had remarkable results; for the continued use of this statement is a powerful force acting and builds a condition in which everything blesses you.

*Warning:* I tell you, you cannot imagine until you get the Freedom of the Inner Vision, what a few moments of inharmonious thought will draw you into, in an unexpected moment.

*This is another reminder:* Say to your outer self: *"You know the Law. This is the wrong thing to do. You must obey if you want me to help you."* Often, it takes just a little encouragement and Inner Radiation to give the Inner Strength to rise out of a thing. The difficulty with Students, as a rule, is that they do not grab a thing quickly enough; for the first and most important thing is to refuse it admittance.

Individuals are so prone to look at the outer things as so important and tangible, when the Inner things are far more tangible.

*The Tangible Presence of the Ascended Masters:* There has been a very sincere desire on the part of a number of Students, to experience Our Tangible Presence; but just because they do not see Us, is no reason they do not feel Our Tangible Presence. We are just as tangible as you are to each other, but the Students do not qualify the Idea of Us with that same tangibility. We are here, but it is your consciousness that has not yet opened the Door. When you enter the Conscious Path, you must have more Faith. You must have Conscious Knowing, Conscious Qualifying—for you are the one at the helm.

*Mastery—get this hint:* When one feels the "Presence," if one would instantly qualify that feeling with the Idea of the Tangible, Visible "Presence," it might do wonders. No mastership is ever gained without this. There is a constant need of recognizing that each one is the person who is qualifying this Energy. *Mastery means continual Conscious Command of Perfection.* You must take the reins now. There is no reason in the world that you should not all have Perfection in your physical bodies—right now.

For any human being on Earth to think that God will intrude His Perfection when the individual is constantly generating and using negative and destructive forces, is perfectly preposterous.

Destructive force is a form of positive force, while negative force but opens the door to some other destructive force than what one has generated for oneself. The destructive force is intensely dynamic. Constructive force is always dynamic and is a thousand times more powerful, for that is its natural element and activity. (This is in regard to a picture flashed to Mr. Ballard's consciousness, in which he was shown an activity that had begun at that time.)

*The destructive activity of thought:* The Ascended Masters have never thought it wise to give forth too much of what takes place through the destructive activity of thought; but I think you and your Students are strong enough to withstand it, and I will say this much: You have all seen the golden sparks in the air. In a fit of anger, resentment, or intense condemnation, the thought clothes that atomic structure about the individual, and nature propels it forth with great force — affecting persons who might unknowingly have their doors open, charging conditions and things to an extent of which they have little conception.

This force generated goes out; and while fragments of it may find lodgment, its accumulation — through momentum — returns and hovers within the etheric atmosphere of its creator. When the above condition is about an individual, is it any wonder that things go wrong with him? That is how some great wrong or crime committed in an environment registers there with great vividness, and is why sensitive individuals going into the place or environment often feel or see — or both — the condition left there.

*Mrs. Ballard:* "I saw Mr. Ballard on the sand at a distance; and after he had been standing still for some moments, he moved away a few steps and stooped down. The place where he had been standing was filled with a Bluish White Light, which did not move over to where his physical body was until some few seconds later."

*Saint Germain:* The Etheric Body does not always move as quickly as the physical, especially when there is a relaxed, harmonious condition of the mind and a feeling of peace. In such cases, it is sometimes quite distinct from the physical.

*Mrs. Ballard:* "I saw a continual movement in the atmosphere as we looked over the lake."

*Saint Germain:* That was the Cosmic Etheric Activity.

*The Love Star:* You cannot give the attention to the Love Star or the Ascended Host without getting a Response. Devotion is a wonderful way to reach through, because devotion is a form of intensified love.

*The Master Jesus and others of the Ascended Host:* While Beloved Jesus and others of the Ascended Host will come forth in Active Service, I think it more powerful for the Students to understand that the coming forth of this Mighty Presence of the Christ, this time, is the Illumining of that "Presence" in the individual—because It is already there.

*Poise:* Poise is really rest. The feelings should always be held in poised restraint. One should watch oneself always for poise in speech, feelings, and action. We should all learn to move quickly, without hurry or irritation; this is poise in action. All Students must acquire this at some time, for they become the embodiment of controlled force.

In all Students' lives, there come times when an occasion demands speedy action; and if one is acting with poise, the mind does not become confused. Then the Inner Direction can come forth with Its attendant ability to do whatever is required. In this way the feelings are kept quiet and the mind clear to receive its right Direction and carry it out.

This is why sensitive individuals naturally, in doing work in the outer where there is no noise or confusion about them, accomplish a great deal scarcely knowing that they are doing it. The vibratory action of noise strikes the mental atmosphere, creating disturbance; and unless the consciousness takes control of it, it causes a leak in the marvelous Stream of Energy flowing.

*BENEDICTION:* Mighty Presence of God! We give praise and thanks for Thy Gracious Outpouring today, for the Radiant Host that are giving of Their Life, Healing, Poise, Wisdom, and Power in great unending Streams to the sincere Students who are looking to the Light. We thank Thee.

# DISCOURSE XXVII

## ARCTURUS' SEMIANNUAL VISIT

*July 4, 1933*

SAINT GERMAIN

*INVOCATION:* Thou Infinite Presence of all Love, Power, and Freedom! We bow before Thy Great Majestic Throne. This symbolizes America's Freedom — the Freedom of all Children of the Earth in the Cosmic Radiation of the "Mighty I AM Presence," whose seed is being planted in the minds of mankind.

So shall all be raised into that Higher Consciousness of True Freedom, Unselfishness, Love, and Adoration to God for the Great Privilege of Life. As the True Understanding of Life means and is God in Action, so may all mankind feel the Sacred Privilege of the Use of Life, and conform to that Harmonious, Loving, Adoring Consciousness of their Source and of each other — thus enabling the True and Mighty God Power to reign in all Activity, as was intended in the beginning.

Thou Mighty Arcturus! We welcome Thee, that

Thy Wisdom through Thy Mighty Radiation shall bless mankind, enlighten and uplift them.

## THE DISCOURSE

ARCTURUS

In this Activity that for some years has taken place for the Blessing of America, We from the Higher Vision see the mighty changes that are taking place. While it is as yet but partially manifest in the outer activity of mankind, yet from the Inner Standpoint there is the steady forward movement that means the certain release of sincere individuals from the binding power of limitation.

This day there has taken place the Activity of the Three Times Three, and of the Seven Times Seven. For seven weeks, Seven Cosmic Rays will govern, consciously directed by Seven Beings from out the Great Central Sun. These will be held at various Points of Focus in the United States to strengthen, to bless, and to adjust that activity of mankind which is necessary to their quickening and further progress. It is not only necessary, but it is commanded to be done.

Seven other Rays are focused — one in England, one in France, one in Germany, one in Italy, one in South America, one in Mexico, and another in

Alaska. It is hoped by this to bring about the necessary adjustment and harmonization in international activity. It is only now that those in authority in America are beginning to awaken to the fact that, heretofore, they were being made pawns of and moved about by a force they did not understand, and caused to do things that they would afterward regret. This is making possible Accomplishments which We scarcely hoped for as possible.

It has been most gratifying to Us to have been able to use the "Century of Progress" as a focal point where all nations of the Earth send their representatives. So, you will understand that the "Century of Progress" Activity was not just an idea in the outer mind of a few men, but holds a deep underlying Purpose that is being utilized to its utmost. Great Ones from Venus, through Their Balance of Love and Power, are giving Great Assistance.

*Private:* Thursday, July 3, 1933, at twelve midnight there began a great Gathering in the Retreat at the Royal Teton. Try to put your bodies to rest by eleven o'clock so that you may participate and witness the Use and Power of the All-Seeing Eye, which has been only put into operation once every hundred years. [Note: In the present cycle, the Outpouring of the All-Seeing Eye takes place every six months, in January and July.] This Retreat is the only place where this particular Activity takes place for reasons that you will one day know and understand. Oh, that mankind might understand the importance of holding themselves within the Harmonious Activity of thought and feeling, knowing that only in this manner can the Fullness of God's Power act. This would hasten so much the things that are to be accomplished.

*To Donald:* My Son, as you appreciated the aerial navigation and activity yesterday, yet will you see such transcendent activity of that kind in the coming years that you can scarcely believe possible at this time. As the power of political selfishness is broken down, it will release into use improvements, inventions, and discoveries in all lines that will step up the progress of such industries from one to two and three hundred years.

The activity of the sinister force that spread its subtle suggestions among mankind, is fast being dissipated; and We trust another war that was being contemplated will be dissipated before it can find action in the outer world.

Never in the history of mankind has such power for good been placed in humanity's hands to use, as the Power from the "Mighty I AM Presence." While this Nucleus of the intense Activity and Idea of this "Presence" seems small indeed, yet is Its Radiance spreading beyond your fondest human conception. The Students who with determination continue to hold fast to the "Presence" and to Its Use, shutting out from the human sense all human, self-created limitation, will come to know a Freedom — a Power to radiate and project that Freedom to bless all with Its Power, in such magnitude as the outer cannot yet possibly comprehend.

It is only because the Wheels of Cosmic Progress have reached a point of Universal Rhythm, that stupendous Activities for the benefit of mankind are possible.

*Warning:* The individuals who become channels for destructive expression are unfortunate indeed; for not only do they destroy themselves, but they deceive their followers, leading them into the quicksands of misconception. I want you to know that I congratulate Saint Germain on the Work that He has accomplished among these few Students, and upon the remarkable manner in which He has enabled them to become aware of and use the Energy of the "Mighty I AM Presence." He said it would be accomplished and He is proving it true. How the Students are blest who are receiving this Knowledge! I trust they may fully appreciate and comprehend It. How unfortunate are those who doubt Its reality or authenticity. More and more necessary is it for you to draw the Seal of Harmony about yourselves and your home, so that the Loving Harmony keeps the channel clear.

Great changes are taking place within the currents of the waters of the Earth; and for the first time within the history of its creation it is possible to harmonize the Activity of the waters and the land. Each of these bodies gives forth a vibratory action as yet not understood, but which will ere long come to be known and utilized; and truly can it be said now, more than ever before, that all things are truly working together for good.

Thou Mighty Seven Cosmic Rays that are doing Thy Work within the Sphere of Earth! In Thy Radiance of Pure Love, fill all the Earth, its waters, its air, its ethers, consuming the mental creation of mankind which they have generated for so many centuries—yea, cycles of time—so that the humanity of Earth may find its outer mind freed from the impact of its own creation—so that they may turn and go forth in Adoration of their own Great Light, the "Mighty I AM Presence," and there receive into themselves Peace on Earth, Goodwill to man. With all the Love of My Being I send this forth, not only in this record but in the Singing Record of the Ethers, to reach the Heart of mankind and lift it in Harmony to its Source, that it may bless and be a Blessing.

I am very pleased to have been with you again and to see how it is possible for you to generate enough love and determination to stand against the impact of the outer world and voice the Truth that makes all free. You know you must acknowledge a thing before you can receive it. Put all doubts of the outer mind aside and whip the human into obedience, and you will see abundant progress.

The outer self of human beings is the most stubborn of creatures. The human creation, by its demand for attention to the outer mind and body, holds its control; and this stubbornness has to be broken up. Each has within his or her "I AM Presence," the Power to put down all human creation and compel it into obedience to the "I AM Presence."

I shall now turn the Ray over to your Beloved Master and shall be with you again the first of the year. My Radiation is a Balancing of the Heart and the Head, or Love and Power. It is quite similar to Chananda's. In regard to the Class, My Work is Cosmic while His is Individual. The time has arrived when the humanity of Earth must come to a greater sense of Balance between those two Activities. The intellect of mankind in official positions has run away more and more, shutting out the Feeling of the Heart that would enable them to consider It and enable greater justice to be done. Chananda's Work with the Students in assisting to balance this Activity will enable them to become Invincible against the impact of the outer world. No words can possibly estimate the value of such an accomplishment.

SAINT GERMAIN

*Question:* "What relation do the constellations have to the Elohim?"

*Saint Germain:* A constellation is, of course, much less than the Power of the Elohim. It is, in other words, much stepped down from Their Activity. But an advanced, consciously operating Being or Individual from any one of the Spheres of Activity is consciously in contact with the Elohim.

The individuals or Students who will hold steadfast enough to the "I AM Presence," will find themselves able to go forth, observe these greater Inner Activities, and bring Them forth consciously into their use. When you see through the Activity of a thing, you then have a full comprehension of it.

The "I AM Presence" has the Fullness of all Activity within Its Consciousness; but in order to bring It forth, the individual must, in most cases, have some use of the Inner Vision to release the Fullness of Its Activity.

*Use the "I AM" Statements of Jesus often: " 'I AM'
the Open Door to all Revelation!" " 'I AM' the Resurrection and the Life!"* So if "I AM" the Resurrection and the Life, what else is there to take place in
your Life? If you can enter into this with steady,
calm certainty, you will find definite changes taking
place.

" *'I AM' the All-revealing Presence of the Great
'I AM'!"*

" *'I AM' the Light that lighteth every room I go
into!"*

" *'I AM' the Discriminating Activity of the Great
'I AM Presence'!"*

We have long since learned not to pay any attention to appearances, but to go into the Heart of
things and there rest.

*Use often: " 'I AM' the ever-present Healing
Power consuming all things that tend toward discord!"*

" *'I AM' the Invincible Presence and Protection
about her or him, wherever the body is!"*

I shall leave My Love and Blessing "sizzling" all
about you.

*The All-Seeing Eye Activity at the Retreat:* It is a
Tremendous combined Activity at the Retreat. You
may know It is of very great importance because of
the shorter length of time between the Outpourings.

*BENEDICTION:* Beloved Nada, Cha Ara, Chananda, Leto, and Cha Ara's Mother (Meta) send Their Love and Blessings to you and also to the Class.

# DISCOURSE XXVIII

## ARCTURUS' DISCOURSE
### ON THE
### MUSICAL FESTIVAL AT SOLDIER FIELD

*August 19, 1934*

ARCTURUS

It is Saint Germain's request that I voice to you the Mighty Accomplishment at the Music Festival last night.

May I first refer to My own Humble Efforts in conjunction with those at the Royal Teton on New Year's Day two years ago. It was then decreed that the Century-of-Progress Exposition should be a Focus for a constructive activity, which should ever expand and increase in intensity during the next one hundred years. The opening and lighting of it was the Initiatory Step that is to usher in the beautiful, magnificent Golden Age which is signalized in that activity.

This has made Soldier Field sacred ground — a Sacred Altar of Divine Activity in the Western World; and so far as humanity at large is concerned, the hub of the whole of America.

A volume could be written on all that took place and that which led up to last evening; but owing to the human sense of time, this must be greatly condensed and but an outline given.

Before proceeding with this description, I wish to call your attention to the unparalleled number of pageants of all kinds, of many nationalities, that are being held in Soldier Field this summer. These cover the period from the Ascension of Jesus down to the present time. They give acknowledgment to the Ascension which is the most vital thing and the culmination of all human experience. These pageants from the human standpoint are a calling forth of the latent memory in humanity at large and are a raising of the Essence of that activity.

How easy it is for humanity to pass over transcendent activities because of their unbelief, their lack of acknowledgment or acceptance of the True Perfection of Life; for all Life in manifestation is *God in Action*. Unfortunately, however, it is more often colored by human concepts of limitation and destructive qualities, which—through the individual's power of Free Will—everyone is at liberty to do. This ere long, however, will be greatly remedied by the setting aside of the greater part of the human Free Will, as it is known today. This will enable much of humanity to be awakened and saved from its own destruction.

Here may I say that the Students who think they can play with the Great Law, because of their unwillingness to give the necessary Self-discipline, will find themselves unfortunate indeed if they attempt it when once having entered upon the Conscious Path. The Great Law, which does not discriminate, takes individuals at their words and feelings. Those who think they can escape this are but deceiving themselves.

The coming pageant of the Celts is really of great importance, for it enters into the vibratory action from the time of Jesus up to the present.

The Inner Activity within and above Soldier Field last night, was one of the most Divine Activities since the advent of the Kumaras into the presence of the Earth. Circle upon circle rose above the surface of the Earth and those seated within the Field. The first circle was formed by the Members of the Great White Brotherhood in their Golden Robes, being those whose outer forms have not yet made the Ascension. Next came the Ascended Host of Masters who have made the Ascension. Then came the Angel Devas and seven of the Cherubim. The circle above Them contained four of the Gods of the Mountains, three of whom you know, the other you shall know. Around these were the Archangels of whom the

Archangel Michael was the Director.

Surrounding the Core of Light within the center of the Field, extending for two hundred feet within the Earth and to five thousand feet above, were Saint Germain, Jesus, the Tall Master from Venus, and the Great Divine Director. They were the Dispensers of the Mighty Currents of Energy sent to all parts of the Earth to do Their Work with no uncertainty.

During the singing of the "Holy City," the Divine Pattern of that which is to become the Holy City upon Earth was lowered into Its position, where It shall remain until It becomes a visible, vibrant City of Light to the westward. The exact position of this I may not disclose at the present time, but I assure you, It was a Mighty Activity which will become a Mighty Reality to the humanity of Earth.

During Mr. Thomas's solos, that great vibratory action was taken up and re-echoed by a great Majestic, Celestial Chorus, whose Radiance poured forth over America like a glistening Shower of Light to consume and bless. During the singing of the Hallelujah Chorus, the entire activity was turned over to the direct dispensation of Jesus Himself.

I wish to assure you that the set pieces in color were not just a human idea; but those responsible for their presence were inspired by the Ascended Masters, principally Saint Germain, in order to establish their renewed, powerful activity which was intensified a thousandfold or more to again act within the Life, the Soul, the Light—from the Heart to the periphery of America and the World.

The representation of signing the Declaration of Independence was to bring before the conscious attention of the Earth and especially America, its unparalleled activity upon the Earth; and *to call it to the attention of the people of America, that they might hold close to and stand by the original Constitution of the United States, which was and is a Divine Creation,* until such time as the complete Ascended Master Constitution of the United States of America shall come forth, as the advance of the Golden Age proceeds.

The Golden Eagle and the Shield represent the Height of Divine Protection for America again reestablished. The Bell of Liberty in the Power color of blue represents the Glorious Liberty and Freedom forever for America and the Earth, from all human selfishness—the instigator of which in every case is private profit. The cause has been the same throughout the ages.

The four powerful Blue Rays that formed a canopy over the Field, thought to be ordinary by the mass of humanity, represented the Fourth Dimensional Activity brought into visibility upon Earth; and *if it be necessary for the Protection of America, the Jewel in the Heart of God, then that Blazing Light as of a Thousand Suns shall descend upon Earth and consume all human inharmony and selfishness from the Planet.*

The fan of Pink Light at the beginning was qualified to serve in the entire Activity; and the Great Love Star stood above all, shedding Its Rays through tier above tier of Great Beings.

I congratulate you and this Good Brother and those many Students of our Beloved Saint Germain; and I thank you all for your earnest, sincere Work on behalf of the Freedom of America. May the Activity of these beloved Students of Light ever continue to expand until from this Nucleus, the Light of Its Radiance covers America.

I also congratulate our Beloved Saint Germain for His great Accomplishment in establishing this Nucleus and Focus in America; and *for His wonderful Love, His Light, His Work for America for nearly two hundred years, which ere long will begin to bear fruit of such perfect kind as has not been heretofore in any civilization.*

I bow in acknowledgment of His great Love, Wisdom, and Strength. I congratulate you, My Beloved Sister and Brother, for your love, steadfastness, patience, and activity for the Students that have been and those that are to follow. Ever know that " *'I AM'* *the only acting 'Presence,'* " and you will find that *all* activity will conform to the *Perfection of that "Presence."* I bid you adieu but not good-bye.

SAINT GERMAIN

Your attention last night was called to an Activity of the Great White Brotherhood in which the Eucharistic Congress was used as an example for that which may follow many times in the future. The representative of the Pope, Cardinal Bonzano of Rome, did make the Ascension from Soldier Field in 1926, in a way not heretofore described. However, it is hoped that this description may be given in the next year or possibly two years. Cardinal Bonzano was and had been for many years, the Representative of the Great White Brotherhood.

The Golden Light never affected anyone's brain except in a harmonious manner, and to illumine and perfect it. It is time to take the nonsense out of the human. There cannot be two masters. Always use the Golden Light on the brain; everybody's brain needs a "Light bath" every day. The average individual only uses about five percent of his or her brain. When you begin to call forth your Eternal Divine Memory, then the vastness of Infinity is in your grasp. If you want Conscious Association with the Ascended Masters, this human has to obey. You have to clean house and not give it its own way under any circumstances. You have to flay it alive until it does only the Will of the "Mighty I AM Presence."

Treat the brain for the Eternal Divine Memory. If you forget something, it is because there is not enough Light in the brain. Treat the mind for clear, calm Ascended Master Comprehension. It is you who must take your mind in hand and tell it how to behave. If you will let it, it wastes tons of energy. Take your brain in hand and command it to be filled with My Ascended Master Consciousness, the Eternal Divine Memory of God.

One with God is the Law. Move forward and walk in It. You will have a tremendous sense of Freedom within yourself if you will do this: Take about ten minutes each day, sit down, and talk to your "Mighty I AM Presence" something like this: " *'Mighty I AM Presence,' listen, You take out of me all criticism, condemning blame, resistance, judging, rebellion, jealousy, self-pity, pride, selfishness, doubt, and fear. Take them out of me and annihilate them, and put Saint Germain's Self-control and Dominion in their place.* " Be as faithful as you can to the healing of the distress of the physical body, but remember to spend most of your time on healing the wounds of hate.

Seven of the Ascended Host, acting from the Violet Temple of Light, sent forth Its Mighty Rays, commanding Obedience to the Inner Activity of forces everywhere acting on the physical plane. Those who can joyously accept the Truth of this Great Activity will receive very great benefit.

All acceptance of the Mighty Truth by the Student must always be voluntary. The more intense the joyous reaching out for Light and Understanding, the more is It hastened into activity in the individual's Life and world. The more one accepts the Inner Truth as a Reality, the more that one can be used as a Mighty Messenger of the Light.

Much is to be given of this Inner Truth that will strain the credulity of even the most sincere Student, so that nothing but the Inner prompting of the individual's own God within will make it possible for him or her to accept it. Nothing will be given except verifiable Truth; yet there will be many who will think some things farfetched, but that is unfortunate for them. No longer in the Mighty Radiation of this Inner "Presence" is the growth of the individual to be considered, but the Radiation will pour forth, clothing humanity in Its Radiation and holding even those without conscious understanding in Its close Embrace.

When you command as the Christ, you cause the

Inner Activity to take place which shuts out the outer. As you continue to fill your mind and body full of God, you are building an Invincible Armor.

The Radiation from the blue costumes at the Music Festival was very powerful because the Blue Ray was used intensely. The Blue Ray is always used to disintegrate the coarser or lower human element.

Lanto is always in charge of the Retreat at the Royal Teton. You will find during the next seven years specific Activity among the Ascended Masters. Those having Special Qualities will be called upon for specific Activity because of Their own Natural Quality.

*Notes to the Students by Mrs. Ballard:* "Say: ' "Mighty I AM Presence," take me to one of the Great Music Temples! Let me hear the Music of the Spheres and see that I record It and bring It back in the morning.' "

*Mr. Ballard:* "There is only one thing to be concerned about—know the 'I AM' is so marvelous that only Its Perfection can express. With all the Love of the Great 'Presence' I say: 'Bless these loved ones that they may be enabled to make within their own mental and feeling world, that condition which is required that will give them, if only once, a manifestation that will forever satisfy them fully.'

"I want to say a word right here. I want to tell

you, if you knew the nights that child [Mrs. Ballard] has stayed up all night long, working for these Students, pouring out the love of her being to you — when she talks about Discipline it is for us to get up and on the job. Saint Germain has put her through a Discipline that many of you would not be able to endure."

*Mrs. Ballard:* "Don't let your mind ever again tell you about anything but the Freedom and Perfection of the 'Mighty I AM Presence.' In your Hearts you do desire to be free. This outer self stands in the way until we whip it into shape. Anyone under Saint Germain's Radiation can succeed in anything he or she desires."

*BENEDICTION:* Out of the Glory of Thy Wondrous Presence, O "Mighty I AM," We feel, We know the Glory of Thy Radiance, Perfection, Health, Joy, Happiness, Courage, and Confidence filling the mind and body of each one of these Beloved Students, filling it so full of Thy Mighty Perfection that there isn't room for a single thing except Thee, and that Thy Marvelous Activity is Eternally Sustained. By the Action of the "Mighty I AM Presence," so fix the Courage, the Confidence, and the Power of the Ascension within the consciousness, that it lifts the consciousness above the binding effect of human things and sets all free in the Full Activity of the

"Mighty I AM Presence" in whatever they are doing.

Oh, "Mighty Presence," how deep Our gratitude that Thou art the only "Presence" and Intelligence acting. Teach each one of the Students to maintain that Love and Peace and Harmony within their consciousness, because only in that can Thy Perfection come forth. Teach the outer to become calm, at peace, and poised in its activity, for all Eternity is before Us. Let Us be grateful and satisfied, and let Us be patient until the Fullness of that "Mighty I AM" is manifest.

Glorify these beloved ones, O Great Ascended Masters of Light, Love, and Wisdom! Glorify them! Enfold them in Thy Wondrous Mantle of Peace, Love, and Light. Clothe them with Thy Mantle. Protect and hold them so close within Thy Embrace, that no human thought enters to mar the Beauty, the Perfection of Thy Wondrous Radiance which Thou art. Glorify each one in that Light, expanding and filling the body with Its Pure, Mighty Energy, Courage, Confidence, and Perfection. Glorify each one with that Perfection which transcends all human concepts, and sets each one free in Beauty, Perfection, and Service of the Light.

(The portion of this Discourse by Arcturus is published in Volume III.)

## SERIES